This Childhood of Mine

*A Memoir of My Last Summer
with My Mentally Ill Mother and Alcoholic Father*

LAURA MEER BARKLEY

PUBLISHING

Copyright © 2024 Laura Barkley
All rights reserved.

No part of this book may be reproduced or transmitted in any form or by any means, electronic or mechanical, including photocopying, recording, or by an information storage and retrieval system—except by a reviewer who may quote brief passages in a magazine, newspaper, or on the web—without permission in writing from the publisher.

Author: Laura Meer Barkley
Publisher: Laura Barkley
Damascus, Maryland, the United States of America

Library of Congress Control Number: 2024924552

First edition (audiobook available)

Cover design by Lynn Andreozzi
Interior design by Furkan Süperdoğan

Contact the author: laurabarkleyy@gmail.com

Ebook ISBN: 979-8-9910996-0-8
Paperback ISBN: 979-8-9910996-1-5
Hardcover ISBN: 979-8-9910996-2-2
Audiobook ISBN: 979-8-9910996-3-9

Author's Note

Dear reader, thank you for choosing my story and going on this journey with me!

I wrote this book about my childhood in Russia to re-experience my past, to reunite with my loved ones, and to heal. The therapeutic effect of writing this book was immense and immeasurable. I hope this book will also help others who had difficult childhoods to forgive, to heal, and, ultimately, to be free to love and thrive.

I wished to give as accurate an account of my life story as possible. The dialogues and sequence of events were reconstructed to the best of my memory. Most names and details of the persons involved were changed to protect their privacy.

Acknowledgments

I'd like to express my deepest appreciation to Kirtland Eastwood, my beta listener, to whom I read my first draft in 2019; to Victoria Lewis, my beta reader; to Elena Vega, Stacey Adkison, and Kristin Kag, my editors; and to Rebecca Allen, my proofreader; for their uncanny understanding of my story and my writing style.

Dedication

*For my beloved daughter **Amina**,
for whom I started writing this book.*

*And for all the kids with difficult lives out there.
I pray God sends them superheroes of their own.*

Contents

Author's Note	3
Acknowledgments	5
Dedication	7
Chapter One An Imperfect Family	11
Chapter Two Sunrise After Dark	19
Chapter Three Cute Babies	33
Chapter Four Another Summer Day to Play	51
Chapter Five Bad Business	69
Chapter Six Father's Wisdom	79
Chapter Seven A Dream Come True	91
Chapter Eight Monsters	101
Chapter Nine Saviors	113
Chapter Ten Good and Bad	131
Chapter Eleven Mother's Intuition	145
Chapter Twelve Back to School	161
Chapter Thirteen A Spy	167

Chapter Fourteen A Star	183
Chapter Fifteen Forgetting to Say Goodbye	195
Chapter Sixteen Daddy Is Asleep	207
Chapter Seventeen Mother or Father	217
Chapter Eighteen The Loneliest Girl in the World	227
Chapter Nineteen Responsible Adults	241
Chapter Twenty A Superhero of My Own	251
Chapter Twenty-One Scary Illusions	267
Chapter Twenty-Two Melancholy	281
Chapter Twenty-Three God Loves Me	289
Epilogue Happily Ever After	295

An Imperfect Family

I'm sitting in my father's room, reading the book *The Rich Also Cry*, easily imagining all the scenes in my head. I've already seen them on TV in the Mexican soap opera of the same name. Mariana and Luis Alberto love each other so much that they overcome all the obstacles life throws at them.

I race to the last page, feeling sad that my virtual journey is going to be over soon. The characters are so lucky to be in love. It must be amazing. I'm only ten now, so I'll have to wait till I'm eighteen to fall in love. But . . . will anyone fall in love with me? *No, I'm unlovable.*

I lift my head and look through the sprawling, unframed window of our glass balcony. The purple sky throws dim light through it, and I can see the shadowed mountains in the far distance. Several palm branches are brushing against the rusty safety bars installed around the balcony. Everything is beautiful tonight.

I lean back in the armchair, lift my mug of black lemon tea from the end table, and sip it slowly. Sugary and delicious but cold. I place the mug back on the table and look around the room, which is actually supposed to be a living room, but Dad converted it into his bedroom because he liked its vastness.

Cigarette butts overflow from ashtrays around the room. Several empty vodka bottles are half lying, half standing in the corner. Spiders, big and small, are crawling on the walls, weaving their webs to catch unfortunate flies. The unpleasant smell of mold is overwhelming.

If only we had money for home renovations. I once bought five lottery tickets, but none of them were winners. Now I know that all the sellers of lottery tickets are swindlers. Either that, or I'm the unluckiest kid on the planet. A weird shiver runs up my back. *I am the unluckiest kid on the planet.*

I sigh. My parents' salaries are no help either—too small. Dad works as a watchman at an accounting company and spends his salary on vodka. And Mom works at a tea plantation and spends her salary on food, toys for me, and other stuff. It's usually all gone in a few days.

My gaze stops on our black-and-white TV set. Dad found it in a street dumpster and fixed it, but then it caught on fire on New Year's Eve, ten minutes before the clock struck twelve. I hope that the folk proverb saying, "The way you meet the new year will be the way you spend it," is wrong.

I look at the floor. It's rotting through. The wood promises to crack at any moment and dump us down to the family of rats living in the tiny basement below. I wanna jump on the chandelier each time I see one of the rats that has dared to come up.

Suddenly, a loud, high-pitched scream cuts through my thoughts. *My mother.* A spasm of fear grips my whole body, and I jerk. The book bounces from my knees and lands loudly on the floor. I jump to my feet.

Mom is running through the corridor, and Dad is chasing after her with a knife in his hand.

"I'm going to kill you, bitch!" Dad shouts.

A cough rises in my throat. "D-D-Daddy, stop!"

Neither of my parents even glances at me. I feel like I'm three years old again, witnessing Dad attacking Mom for the first time. I'm helpless and paralyzed and confused. This time their fight seems worse because Dad is holding a knife. *Oh, what to do?*

I watch in horror as Mom bursts into the bedroom she and I share, and Dad runs after her, slamming into her back from behind. Both of them then tumble down onto my bed. Dad raises the knife over Mom's neck.

A shooting pain grips my temples, making me move. I run toward the bedroom, leaping over the threshold and jumping on Dad's back. I start pummeling him with my fists with all my might. He still doesn't feel me, being so focused on my mother. It's only when I grab the handle of the knife that he freezes.

"Oh, shit," he mutters, and a familiar, acrid smell from his mouth fills the room. Vodka. *He's drunk again.* How didn't I notice that earlier when we were talking? He was a bit sad, yes, but that's all.

"Can you please hide the knife, Dad?" I ask him softly.

"S-sorry," he stammers, getting to his feet. "Yes, yes."

He's such a giant, the tallest dad in our neighborhood. He makes our bedroom tiny, though he's not particularly wide—his muscles are quite lean. I stare at him as he hides the knife behind his back and retreats into the corridor.

"Don't tear your pants," I tell him.

I rush to the door and lock it, looking at Mom. She's huddled in the corner of the bed, shivering. My vision blurs. Why do my parents hate each other so much? Either Mom shouts at Dad, or he tries to kill her. He even told me once that one day my mother would be in a grave, he in prison, and I in an orphanage.

I've seen Mom jump out the window to meet her lovers at night, but he doesn't know about that. Is it their age difference of twenty-two years? I don't think so.

"Turn the lights on," Mom tells me, jolting me back to the present.

I nod and turn to press the switch on. The small room fills with yellow light, so warm, so happy. I like our chandelier very much, as it reminds me of the sun.

Mom grabs a ball of blue woolen yarn and her knitting needles and starts to weave her magic with my future winter sweater. I take a few seconds to study her. She has short, strawberry-blond hair, narrow eyes, and flower-shaped lips that my mind associates with her endless kisses.

"I'll go check on Dad," I say.

"It's not your job, Laura!" Mom says sharply.

"I know, but I, uh . . ."

"If you must."

I head to Dad's room. He's taking off his gray shoes and lying down on his coffee-colored couch. As if nothing has happened. He just looks tired.

The sky through the window is pitch black now. It went from purple to this color in just . . . what? The fight seemed to last forever, but in actuality, it took no more than a minute.

I look back at Dad. "Let's go to the beach and collect bottles."

His lips move weakly. "Kiddo, I need to sleep a bit."

"OK," I agree. Sleep will be good for him.

"I'll wait for you in the kitchen," I say, exiting the room and closing the door.

I sprint across the corridor to the kitchen, scaring all the cockroaches into running away.

"There, there," I whisper jokingly.

"Are you coming in?" Mom yells from the other side of the wall.

"No," I yell back. "I'm going to the beach with Dad."

"Be careful. Many people want to kidnap you because you're beautiful."

"Don't be ridiculous," I snap. Then, feeling guilty, I add apologetically, "But my hair is beautiful."

I touch the curls. After begging Mom for days to make my hair look bouncy like the hair of *The Rich Also Cry*'s heroine, she finally borrowed hair rolls from a neighbor and wound my hair.

"I'm going to bed early," Mom yells again.

"Are you alright?" I ask, alarmed.

"I won't be until that drunkard is in jail."

I cringe at her words. I hope Dad didn't hear them. If he did, he might become mad again. I wait. Nothing, thankfully.

Relaxing, I sit at the kitchen table, push all the jars aside, and get my art album with pencils. Spreading them out on the table, I go to work. I don't have a Barbie doll, but I can draw her and her outfits and then color them.

"The pink dress is the best," Dad says, shuffling into the kitchen.

"Oh, you're already up," I squeal with joy.

He rubs his eyes. "I've been asleep for two hours."

His lips look purplish.

"I think you need some coffee. Want me to make it?"

"We don't have any," he says with a wry smile.

"Let's ask a neighbor to lend us some."

"Too late."

"Tea instead?"

"Just water," Dad wheezes, turning on a faucet, then he says, "Take a sweater with you."

"No need, I never get cold. And I don't get colds either." Besides, today I have on my favorite white eyelet lace dress. I don't want to cover it with anything.

"Our beloved God is watching over you," Dad comments.

I look at him. Does he mean that's why I never get sick? I smile. That sounds nice. I like it. Imagining that someone so magical and powerful is watching over me, protecting me, is exhilarating.

Dad clears his throat. "Are you hungry?"

"No," I answer. "Don't worry. Mom cooked farina porridge earlier today."

Dad takes me by the hand, and we walk out into the entrance hall, then continue to our courtyard. Our destination is the beaches on the other end of our street. We're so lucky to live in the paradise of Sochi, the most famous resort city in Russia. It'll take us just five to ten minutes to reach the central beach.

I look up at Dad's almost silver hair. The bald spot on his scalp has disappeared. That means iodine really helps to treat shingles, just as his doctor promised.

I start skipping to the rhythm of songs in my head. I move fast, getting far ahead of Dad. The crickets seem to be following me around. I slow down and leap from one streetlamp to another, from one spotlight on the asphalt to another.

Our Voykova Street is so quiet at night. During the day it's hustling and bustling with people, especially in summers, when the Black Sea is warm and around five million tourists visit our small city of only three hundred thousand citizens. The tourists walk around and rap on the doors in the apartment buildings, asking the owners to rent them a room. Some of my neighbors put signs on their doors, saying, "We are not renting our rooms."

When I reach the seafront, I stop and wait for Dad so we can enter the beach together. The moment we step on the pebbles, happiness overwhelms me. The smell of the salt in the air, the feel of the gentle breeze against my skin, and the sound of the foamy waves are soothing. The visual of one bright strip of moonlight crossing the sea and washing over our faces is dazzling.

"The sky is full of stars tonight," Dad notes.

I look at him sideways. What else does he need to be happy?

"Why won't you stop drinking?" I ask and immediately bite my lip.

An anguished expression comes over his face. "I just can't."

Feeling a surge of pity, I turn away. I can't watch his soulful blue eyes glisten with tears. *Poor Daddy.*

Chapter Two
Sunrise After Dark

Shortly after 4 a.m., the sun slowly rises, coloring the sky in all shades of candy pink. Early morning is my favorite time. The birds are singing in an overpowering orchestra, and flowers open their petals.

Dad and I have wrapped up our job for today. Our bag is full of empty bottles we found scattered all over the beaches. Tourists are sometimes too lazy to go to the trash cans. Easier for us. Now we can sell the bottles to a recycling center.

"How much will we get for them?" I ask Dad.

"Just enough to buy some sausages, a loaf of bread, and milk," he replies.

I nod and focus on the pavement above. The seafront winds up toward the park on the slope. We climb the stairs and walk past expensive hotels and then a concert hall, heading toward a gold-domed church.

"The money will be very good because a pickpocket cut into Mom's purse recently and stole her wallet," I say.

"How much did she have?" Dad asks.

"Her whole salary for the month."

"Did she report him?"

"No, just cried a lot, and a neighbor lent her some money."

"She needs to report that."

"She was at the police station the other day," I say. "She doesn't want to go there again."

Dad tenses, and I hurry to explain. "No, not to report you. A salesperson poured a bucket of cold water on her from the second floor."

Dad furrows his brows. "What happened?"

"My waffle roll didn't have cream in the middle, and Mom went ballistic, accusing the store of swindling us."

I roll my eyes, remembering that day. Why does Mom always have to be so passionate about even the smallest of things? She shouted and shouted at the salespeople, her opera-like voice filling the streets around. I wanted the ground to swallow me. Every store in Russia does that trick with cream. It's no big deal. Those people working in the store were innocent . . . until, that is, one of them went upstairs and did the thing with water. Poor Mom was all drenched.

Dad shakes his head. "Cheating kids is wrong."

"But Mom often overreacts." *To put it mildly.*

Is that a smirk on Dad's face? Oh, he knows how vocal Mom can be.

We stop at one of the street dumpsters, and Dad peeks inside, then rummages through the contents.

"A vinyl record player!" This cry of excitement from him is sudden and shrill.

I perk up and come closer to look at it. "If it doesn't work, I can play with it."

"And there's a big chunk of Doctorskaya bologna, almost a whole stick," Dad says, pulling it out of the trash.

"Is it safe to eat?"

"Hmm . . . we'll boil it for a few hours to kill the germs."

I shrug my shoulders. "I guess."

From the corner of my eye, I notice movement in the calm blue sea below. I turn my head and see that it's dolphins. A school of them is moving along the shore, somersaulting in the air, following each other.

"Dad!" I yell, craning my neck to see better. "Dolphins!"

It's rare to see such a childlike expression on his face. For the first time in ages, he smiles with all his teeth showing.

When the group of gray dolphins disappears from view, Dad takes my hand, and we continue on our way. Now we're carrying additional trophies. I imagine I can play with this record player as if it were a magic drum from the TV game *Field of Miracles*.

Dad and I pass a tree blossoming with fluffy pink flowers. I stop, stick the player under Dad's arm, and run back to the tree to sniff it. Not a lot of scent, but the flowers are silky to the touch. Beautiful.

"I saw your friends riding their scooters down to the main road," Dad says when I catch up with him. "It's dangerous."

"We always turn before the road."

"'We'?"

"They let me use their scooters, yes. Can you buy me one?"

"My love, you know we don't have that kind of money. If I could, I'd buy you anything you want. What else would you have liked to have?"

"A Barbie doll," I answer immediately. "There's nothing I want more."

Dad smiles slowly. "Of course."

As we walk down our driveway toward our courtyard, someone yells out their window, "What's with all the noise? We're sleeping here."

Dad makes a face at me, then shifts the bag of bottles to his other hand to keep it from rattling. I don't know how he thinks it can help.

When we get home, I go to Mom's and my bedroom and fall on my bed, completely exhausted. I watch a small fly walking upside down on the ceiling, and this makes me gradually fall asleep.

My sleep is troubled. I keep waking up. After managing to sleep for a few hours, I jolt awake. Tears are running down my cheeks. I've just had a horrible dream. In it, my mother smiled at me happily, told me she loved me, kissed me on the cheek, said goodbye, then left forever.

Doll and Mickey, our two dogs, jump onto my bed and snuggle up at my side. I stroke their little backs and pull them toward me for kisses. How do they know I'm upset?

Dad's best friend, Runia, gave me Doll when I was in first grade. She was black as coal and very beautiful, so Mom called her Doll. When she grew up and had her own puppy, we called him Mickey because he looked just like Mickey Mouse, white with black ears and a black forehead. I love my dogs.

Metallic clicking coming from the corner of the room draws my attention, and I look up. My mother is sitting in her armchair, knitting. No, not knitting. As I focus on her hands,

I see that instead, she's using a sewing needle to stab through her fingernails and dig out the flesh underneath. I feel my head spin in horror.

I jump up from the bed and shout, "What are you doing?"

"Calm down, Laura," Mom says. "I'm just removing the ticks."

"What ticks?"

"The ticks I got when I was cutting the leaves from the tea shrubs."

I approach her and hover over her fingers. There are absolutely no ticks in her nails.

"Please stop hurting yourself," I plead.

"You don't understand. If I don't get them, they'll multiply. I had them on my face. I know."

"On your face? Mom, you're imagining things."

"Don't undermine me like that," she growls.

"But isn't there an easier way to treat . . . er . . . ticks?" I ask gently.

Mom nods. "School glue. It makes your skin as soft as a marshmallow. You can try it when you're a grown-up."

"No, thank you," I reply dryly. "I'll pass."

Shuddering, I close my eyes. Maybe if I can't see what Mom's doing, it's not actually happening.

I turn away and go to my wardrobe, getting my shorts and a tank top and changing into them. The dogs and I exit the room, then I can't help but glance at Mom one more time. She's smiling, happy. In an instant, her mood changes. She starts crying. I stand there for a time, paralyzed, watching the tears stream down her scrunched face. I take a step toward her, then stop. The dogs have already jumped onto her lap and are trying to soothe her, feeling her distress.

I close the door behind me and go outside. My head aches, and I press my temples with my fingers and look around. The hydrangeas are blooming purple, white, blue, and pink. I sit at one of the bushes and play with the curly flowers. I turn them upside down and imagine they're dolls in the brightest dresses from the last century.

"Laura, it's you!" a small older lady passing by gushes.

"Do you know me?" I ask her. She doesn't look familiar. She has cropped gray hair and a small crimson birthmark on her cheek in the shape of a triangle. No, I've never seen her before.

"Ah, you don't remember me," she states the obvious. "I was your neighbor in the past. And before that, I was a good friend of your grandma Maria."

I nod, though I don't know my grandma either. She died before I was born.

"Don't you feel hot with the shawl on your shoulders?" I ask rudely.

"My mother crocheted it for me when she was alive," she says. "It's my talisman now."

"It sounds sad. Living without your mother, I mean."

She halfway smiles, then her face becomes serious. "I heard you almost gave your neighbors a heart attack when they saw you crawling from rooftop to rooftop of your duplex. Be careful!"

"OK." I shrug.

"I'll be on my way. Say hi to your dad from Mrs. Margar."

As Mrs. Margar disappears from view, I see another older lady walking past me. Half-bent, with a bulbous nose, she reminds me of Baba Yaga, the evil old lady from TV cartoons. I make a mental note not to slouch so my back won't grow hunched like that.

Chiding myself for staring, I turn away. Should I go to someone's garden and pick fruit? Which kind do I want? Pears, apples, plums, loquats? Cherries!

I get up from the ground and sneak into a neighbor's garden with the tallest cherry tree in the neighborhood. The tree is higher than the three-story house it stands next to.

Quietly, I tiptoe to the trunk, wrap my arms around it, and start to climb. It's off-season for cherries, but there are still some deep red, almost brown berries hanging on the upper branches. I reach them in no time, then prop myself on the three sturdiest branches in the shape of a fork and relax. The overripe cherries taste delicious. They burst with juice that's both sweet and tart. I savor each drop.

A little brown sparrow lands on a nearby branch and starts pecking at the cherries, not afraid of me at all. We eat in companionable silence. When I'm full, I pick some cherries for Mom, store them inside my T-shirt, and begin climbing down.

I grab a branch on either side of me and lower my weight to the branch below. Why is it so much scarier to climb down than it is to climb up? I take another step down and another. Just in case, I hug the tree trunk and continue even more cautiously.

Suddenly, a bough I step on snaps, and I begin sliding down the trunk. I don't even have time to get scared, because, just as suddenly, my fall stops. A little branch beneath me caught me. I sit on it, looking at it with gratitude as adrenaline pounds in my ears. I can't believe I was so lucky. *Thank you, Branch. Thank you, God.*

Mrs. Margar has just told me to be careful, and here I am, doing tree-sliding. From now on, I'm going to test every limb of the tree before I lower my full weight onto it.

When close to the ground, I hop down the rest of the way and land on the soft grass below. Then I dump the smashed cherries out of my shirt. Let the small animals eat them.

My shirt is now stained, but who cares? I shake some of the mess off it and head for the courtyard. I can already hear kids' voices coming from it, so I break into a run.

The kids turn out to be my friends, sparkly Nina and her equally sparkly younger brother David. They're making paper planes. I wrap my arms around my body, lean against the plaster wall of our apartment building, and watch the two siblings launch their planes into the air. If I could whistle with surprise, I would—the newspaper planes are gliding, rising over the rooftops.

"Can you make planes?" David asks me in a slightly girly voice. He'll probably outgrow this by the time he's his sister's age.

"Yes," I lie. "I'm good at making planes." *The type that wouldn't fly higher than the first-floor window.*

"Come, show us," Nina says, handing me a newspaper.

I dismiss her offer with a wave of my hand. "It's not good paper. Too soft. When did you get freckles? I didn't know you could have them with brown hair."

She smiles and shrugs.

David, on the other hand, doesn't let the plane question go. "The newspaper worked for us."

Cornered, I grab the offered newspaper, tear a big sheet, and fold it vertically, then make a few sharp lines. *Ready.* Taking a step back, I lift my arm and launch the plane into the air.

It swerves a few short loops pitifully, dips down, and falls at Nina's feet. *Busted.*

"That's OK," Nina reassures me. "My granddad learned how to make paper planes seventy years ago and then taught us."

"Will you teach me?" I ask.

Before she can answer, David interferes. "She won't. It's a family secret."

I wrinkle my face in disappointment but pretend I don't care. Biting the inside of my cheek, I stay silent.

Something makes me glance up, and I see Mrs. Sokol, my favorite neighbor, in one of the small windows on the side of the building. She's watching us. Her dandelion-white hair makes me smile each time I see it.

Does she need me to go buy groceries or to run some errands for her? I should go and ask.

I climb the stairs to the second floor, two steps at a time, and ring the bell of the first door on the left.

I hear Mrs. Sokol shuffling. "Here, here."

"It's me, Laura," I say loudly.

"My dear," she says, opening the door.

"Do you need any help?"

She brushes my shoulder with her hand. "Um . . . can you cut my toenails? I can't reach them, and I'm embarrassed to ask my son."

"Absolutely."

I follow Mrs. Sokol as she wobbles into her room and sits on the bed. I bend and gather crumbs of bread from the floor, then put them on the table. No wonder the apartment smells of bread.

"Thank you," Mrs. Sokol says and gestures toward a small cabinet. "The scissors are there."

I open the lower drawer she points at, take the scissors, and start my work. This thing is too big and heavy for my hand, but somehow I manage to cut the protruding nails from her tiny feet. My work is sloppy, but Mrs. Sokol looks happy with the result.

"Do you remember your dances when you were little?" she asks.

"Vaguely," I reply. "Only my Ducklings and Swans dance."

She gurgles with laughter. "You would choreograph different dances daily for us old ladies. We were your audience."

I shove the scissors back into their drawer. "Anything else?"

"No," she replies and points toward the table at the kitchen entrance. "Take some candies from the vase there."

I eye the vase suspiciously. The last time I got a chocolate bar from it, I found white worms crawling in the filling. *Thank you, no, thank you.*

"I'm on a diet," I lie.

"What diet?" Mrs. Sokol asks, surprise in her voice.

"Uh . . . I was told . . . to eat less sugar."

"But—"

"Nina and David are waiting for me in the courtyard."

"Just stay a little. Tell me some news. It's tedious to be alone all day."

"OK," I agree. "Today I met Mrs. Margar."

"I know her very well!" Mrs. Sokol exclaims. "My husband and her husband served in World War Two together."

"I'm afraid of even hearing about wars."

"Yes, they are tragedies. God save you children from wars. I still remember the horrible starvation. My happiest day was when I found a beet growing in the soil."

"Did you eat it raw?"

"Yes. Now I like it boiled and with ground walnuts. My teeth are missing, you know."

I nod. "And what news do you have?"

"No news at all. But I have a feeling I'm going to join my husband in heaven soon."

"Don't say that!"

Mrs. Sokol looks to be in her nineties, but surely she can live much longer.

She smiles at me indulgently. "Honey, go play outside. I won't keep you any longer."

I don't argue and go out of the apartment, then run downstairs. By now, ten kids have gathered in the courtyard, all from different parts of our neighborhood. I start to play with them, and by early evening there are twenty of us. We have so much fun!

Henry, a newcomer from Tonnelnaya Street, is now aiming a ball at us. We scurry away in different directions.

"Don't accidentally throw the ball over the fence!" I yell at him.

He tosses the ball too high, as if he has pigeon toes or too much strength or a walleye. But he doesn't have a walleye. He and his twin brother have perfectly aligned, clear azure eyes.

Henry suddenly stops at the corner of the building and listens to something with a dumb expression on his face.

"What?" I ask him, raising my hands questioningly.

He lifts a finger to his lips and gestures for all of us to be quiet. "I hear a man and a woman arguing."

I sigh. A man and a woman, yeah, right. I go to the side of the building to confirm that the man and woman are my parents. Once there, I wish I hadn't come.

"Piece of shit!" Mom yells.

"Fuck you!" Dad replies.

Yes, that's them. Dad's voice sounds sober, and when he's sober, he never starts fights first. That means Mom stirred the pot. I purse my lips with irritation.

"You set my fridge on fire, slut!" Dad bellows. Oh, so it wasn't Mom who started the fight.

"And you threw a plate at me and cut my earlobe," Mom bellows back.

"It's Laura's parents," David announces, coming to stand behind me.

I turn to look at him in anger. The little boy that he is, he can't keep his mouth shut. Only the neighbors from our apartment building know that my parents fight all the time. The newcomers didn't have to know.

David shrugs apologetically.

"Let's keep playing," I say and run to the center of the courtyard, trying to divert everyone's attention from my parents.

Matthew, Henry's twin brother, catches up with me and whispers in my ear, "Did your mom really light your dad's fridge on fire?"

Gosh, at least he's more subtle than little David.

"No, she didn't, Matthew," I answer. "The fire was caused by Dad's smoldering cigarette."

I'm amazed I can tell the twins apart. The features of one brother seem to be softer than the features of the other.

"Shouldn't you go check on your parents?" Matthew asks.

"No," I reply. "My mother only shouts at Dad from the safety of our room when it's locked."

Henry, who's come to stand next to us and heard the last part, asks, "Won't he get her tomorrow?" *Curiosity killed the cat.*

"Tomorrow it'll be something else," I reply dismissively.

The brothers shake their heads in a synchronous motion. Are they programmed to do everything together? Thankfully, Ava, my friend and neighbor, saves me from further questioning by throwing her red-and-yellow striped ball at me.

I burst into giggles and run after her. When I throw the ball back, it only touches her fuzzy hair. I run after the ball and now target David, but feeling sorry for the little guy, I turn to chase the others.

"Did Mia already leave for Moscow?" a boy, whose name I don't remember, asks me.

"Yes," I answer, still running around the courtyard.

The boy keeps up with me, his dark green sandals squishing from the effort. Did he pee himself?

"Did Mia still have her hair cut in a square?" he asks.

"Yes, and she's more beautiful than ever, with her tiny nose and all," I answer honestly, then ask bluntly, "Are you in love with her?"

"Yes," he answers sheepishly, his eyes glazing over.

I'm not surprised. Every boy in our neighborhood is in love with Mia. She's a pretty brunette with a singsong Moscow accent. Even George, Ava's handsome older brother, is in love with her. I'm jealous of her, but on the other hand, I like her very much—she's good-mannered, friendly, talented, and very kind.

I kick the ball, almost missing it, and everyone starts to laugh.

"You won't become a soccer player," yells the same boy who asked about Mia.

"Will you?" I ask sarcastically.

"No. Let's play pioneer ball instead."

Everyone agrees, and we divide into two teams and start catching the flying ball for the next hour or so. After darkness falls, my companions, one by one, leave for home. Reluctantly, I go home too.

In the kitchen, I grab a bag of flour and mix it with sugar and water, then fry crepes. Simultaneously, I make a cup of hot, sweet tea and sit at the table for my nice dinner.

I postpone going to the bedroom because I don't want to see Mom's nails. But eventually, I have to.

"Why are you sulking?" Mom asks me as I enter our room, avoiding looking at her.

"Sleepy," I lie.

"Would you like me to read you a bedtime story then?"

"Of course!" What a wonderful offer.

"It's *The Tale of Tsar Saltan*," Mom declares in a silky-smooth TV voice, then kisses my temple with a loud smack and sits on the edge of my mattress. "The tale is written by Pushkin."

I settle under my feather blanket comfortably and close my eyes—this way I'll be able to envision everything I hear.

"Three fair maidens," Mom starts reading, "late one night, sat and spun by candlelight. 'Were our tsar to marry me,' said the eldest of the three, 'I would cook, and I would bake. Royal feasts I would make!'"

Chapter Three
Cute Babies

The next day Mom wakes me early and tells me that Kristen, a seven-year-old friend, is waiting for me in the entrance hall. Hooray! Though I still feel groggy. Unsteadily, I get up from my bed, put on my still-damp-after-washing polka-dot jumper, and go out.

"Sorry for waking you," Kristen says, meeting me on the porch. "I need your help. My friend Aisha invited me to her birthday party, but I don't have a gift for her."

"Let me think," I say, lowering myself to the bottom step of the stairs.

How can I refuse to help Kristen? She's a darling of our neighborhood, with her kinky brown hair and long eyelashes.

"Do you have something at home that we could sell?" I ask.

She sits down on the step next to me and stares at my face before answering, "A new pack of woolen tights."

"You'll need them in the winter."

"OK, then. I also have butter that Mom's friend brought us from abroad."

"Butter?" I ask incredulously.

"Yes, but it's in a colorful plastic box."

"Show me," I say, getting up and heading toward her entrance hall.

Kristen's fridge is practically empty. Eggs and that box of butter; that's all. Almost like my fridge. I take the box and turn it around in my hands. Yellow with blue inscriptions in some foreign language. It's 500 grams—big. I open the lid and look inside. There's a dent in the butter from a teaspoon. How will we be able to sell it? I suppose we can say we did a quality test.

"What will you tell your mom about the absence of the box?" I ask Kristen curiously.

"I'll pretend I know nothing about it." She shrugs.

I snort, then shrug too.

We head for the grocery shopping area at the intersection of our street and the next. There are at least ten vendor booths arranged in a circle, selling junk food and alcohol. Looking around to check that there are no acquaintances, I tug Kristen toward the first booth.

"Ma'am," I address the young saleswoman behind the counter. "Would you like to buy this butter? It was imported from abroad."

She shakes her head, then turns away, pretending to be busy with undoing her French braid.

We walk over to the next booth and get our second refusal. At the third booth, the saleswoman opens the lid and looks with confusion at the missing chunk of butter. *Bummer.* She still winks at us when she hands the box back, her eyelashes heavy with mascara. Wishing us luck?

It's at booth number six that we finally get lucky. The saleswoman here gives us a megawatt smile and immediately agrees to buy the butter.

"What's the price?" she asks us.

Oh no, we forgot to discuss the price. I look at Kristen, but she just stares back at me. *Think fast, Laura.* I scan the price tags on the candies sold in the booth, and an idea strikes me.

I turn to the saleswoman. "Let's exchange the butter for your box of Raffaello coconut candies."

"My pleasure," she says, and her flat mouth again stretches into a stunningly wide smile. "And I'll give you a bar of raisin chocolate as a bonus."

"Thank you," Kristen says to her.

I get my own thank you from Kristen when we leave the shopping area, and she makes a sharp turn on her heel to hug me.

I laugh and push her away. "I don't like being thanked. Will Raffaello be a good gift for . . . ?"

Aisha, and yes, it will," she says and hands me the chocolate bar. "It's yours."

"No, break it in two," I protest.

"I'll eat a piece of the birthday cake today."

I smile and take the bar. "Are you going to dress up nicely?"

"I'll wear my new sandals with pink bows and glitter."

I nod. The next time I get money, I'll buy the shoes with one-inch heels I saw in a shop window the other week.

"I don't know which dress to choose yet," Kristen says. "I'll have to look in the mirror to decide."

"Ugh, I don't like to look at my reflection," I say.

"Why? Don't you love yourself?"

"Love myself? Nope." How would that even be possible? I'm disgusting.

"My grandma always says that for others to love you, you should love yourself first."

I scrunch my nose, not getting it. No one will love me whether I do it first or not. Except for my parents, of course.

"I'm going to run now," Kristen says, waving her hand at me. "Don't want to be late."

"See you in the evening, maybe," I say, watching the soles of her shoes flash as she takes off toward our apartment building. A girl on a mission.

I, on the contrary, slow my pace and eat my chocolate in small, square chunks, sucking each piece to prolong the taste of melting cocoa on my tongue. Raisins go well with chocolate.

A car passes me with a loud English song blasting out the open windows. I check that no one's around and start to sing loudly, garbling the unknown foreign words I've just heard. It's so nice to sing freely like this. I should do it more often.

Did I just hear my name? I get quiet and perk my ears. Yes! It's Dad. He's calling for me.

I start running up the hill and up the street stairs, shouting, "I'm here! I'm here!"

Dad sighs with relief as he sees me. "I've been looking for you everywhere. Twenty minutes till the show."

"What show?"

"The circus. I bought us tickets."

"Amazing."

I grab his big hand, and we walk hurriedly down the hill. Our city is all about the mountains and hills, and our apartment building stands right in the middle of one, sparsely surrounded by smaller apartment buildings.

Dad and I cross the main road and run toward the bus stop. The long bus we get on resembles a yellow caterpillar and is just as slow. I take in the sights of the city and count the seconds until we reach our destination. Fortunately, we arrive in plenty of time. Dad even calls for a photographer to take a picture of me on a big gray horse before we buy popcorn and hurry to our seats, which are in the middle row at the front of the arena.

The show starts with a dance by about thirty different performers, all dressed in shiny costumes. I like all the acts that unfold throughout the show, except for the magicians and jugglers—they make me feel a bit bored.

I brighten again when goats come into the arena. They're funny because they don't listen to their middle-aged, wise-looking trainer. In the end, they get loose and scatter about, embarrassing the man thoroughly.

The poodles dressed in fluffy pink skirts that perform next are another story—they're very smart. They do mathematical tricks, jump, and push a stroller with a baby doll.

Then comes a woman with colorful hula hoops. She starts twirling fifty or so of them all at once, skillfully. I don't understand how she does it. It seems pretty impossible.

I move to the edge of my seat. Aerial acrobats are now in the arena. They start flying high in the air, getting higher and higher. All they have for safety is blue ribbons hanging from the ceiling.

"They're a married couple," Dad says, "so the performance is romantic."

"Yes, they look like a princess and prince," I say. "But how do you know they're married?"

He smiles. "The same last name."

"Aren't you Sherlock Holmes?"

The couple's performance becomes increasingly more dangerous, and I desperately hope they won't fall. They don't. They land on the red carpet gracefully, and the audience claps vigorously.

After they leave, a clown with orange hair rides out on a unicycle, using a whistle as his voice. It's funny, and all the small kids laugh.

I sniff the air and look left and right. It seems to me something smells like pee. Could it? My question is answered when a crocodile in the hands of its handler begins peeing on the arena's carpet right from the handler's hands.

Loud trombones start blaring, signaling yet another performance. I look in the direction of the sounds. There are at least ten musicians dressed in formal black suits.

"Look!" Dad pats me on my shoulder. "Bears."

My eyes widen. Three little brown bears clumsily lumber into the center of the arena, walking between their masters. One bear is playing a miniature accordion while two others are dancing with bouquets of flowers. Their paws seem more flexible than I expected. Ah! One of the bears has started to roar.

My palms are red from clapping. I decide not to applaud for a time. No luck. The entrance curtains shift, and two elephants walk out. One of them is very small—a baby. I start clapping again. I want to cry; the baby elephant is so cute.

Both elephants amble around the stage, flapping their ears and wiggling their trunks. The audience squeals with delight. The older elephant starts rolling on the floor, performing tricks, while the baby elephant continues circling the arena, doing nothing, just staring at the audience in the first row adorably.

A teenage boy sitting beside Dad has fallen asleep. I can't believe it. And what's with his torn jeans? Is he poor? Or is it some kind of fashion?

The show ends with all the performers parading into the arena, waving, and then leaving for backstage. Dad and I get up from our seats and file with everyone to the exit.

Outside, clowns in rainbow costumes sell long balloons and show kids how to make animals out of them. A few artists turn kids' faces into animal faces with just a few drops of colorful paint.

"Do you want to hang out here or go home?" Dad asks.

"Go home," I reply.

We catch a bus, ride it to the Musical School stop, then go home along Voykova Street. In the thirty houses we pass, I know nearly every family. For all the kids living on our street, our courtyard is the favorite hangout. It's big and spacious. In summers, there can be as many as fifty of us in the evening, counting the tourist kids.

After a while, Dad asks, "Do you remember the snowman we built here last winter?"

I look around, recalling the spot. "Yes. It was the middle of the night, and Doll played in the snow like a lynx while Mickey was scared of it."

Dad nods and takes my hand as we walk into the driveway. I look at our apartment building. It's off-white and four stories high, with expansive balconies and zigzag stairs connecting it to its twin building, creating a duplex.

Doll and Mickey run out into the courtyard to meet us, stumbling over each other with excitement. Mickey loves me more, but Doll definitely loves Dad more. She once ran on a highway after a bus he was on. Poor thing had to give up when the roar of a motorcycle scared her.

As all of us step into our apartment, Dad asks me to find his large metal samovar for boiling tea so we can sell it at the Central Market. I hurry into his room and start to search. Selling things at the market is one of my favorite pastimes. When I was little, Dad even raised chickens and white rabbits on our glass balcony so we could sell them. But our neighbors started complaining about the odor, and we had to quit our little business adventure.

"You're so pale," Dad says, seemingly to the wall beside him. I stop what I'm doing and stare at him, dumbfounded.

"Was it you who stole my dried fish?" he asks the wall again.

My eyes widen, but before I can think he's talking to a ghost, I see ears sticking from the couch. Mickey! I have to laugh.

I continue looking for the samovar in Dad's mess. This horde of treasures reaches my waist. Dad has gathered so many things from the street dumpsters that I still haven't found the samovar. When I grow up, I'll be a minimalist.

"Laura," Mom shouts from our bedroom. "You're home. Come here, now!"

"Did you need something?" I ask, coming into the bedroom, my voice cracking with worry.

She immediately starts shouting at me. And when she shouts, she's really loud, scary.

"I met one of your school vice principals today," she yells. "She said you'd missed ninety-five percent of the last school year's classes."

The blood drains from my face, and I take a step back. Mom gets up from the armchair and grabs her book of knitting patterns, preparing to hit me with it.

"No, Mom, no!" I shriek, raising my hand in front of my face. "My school satchel was stolen, and I was afraid to tell you. That's why I had to skip school."

I don't say it was stolen from the bushes where I'd hidden it so I could walk the beach and play truant there. And I don't want to say I skipped school to avoid the bullies in my class. Poor Mom tried everything to stop them—she had meetings with the principal, my teacher, and the parents, but nothing helped.

Mom looks at me, puzzled, then scans the room. "No school satchel?"

I shake my head. "No."

"Why didn't you tell me?"

Relieved that she isn't angry with me anymore, I sit on my bed and decide to recount a little bit of what the bullies did to me last year.

"There's another reason I didn't want to go to school," I confide. "The last time I went to school, my classmates stuck my arms with a syringe needle. I showed our teacher the drops of blood on my hands, but she just politely asked them to stop."

Mom's face droops. "You're transferring to middle school now. One of the other vice principals is going to be your homeroom teacher."

"Really?"

"Yes. I'm sure that woman won't allow any bullying."

I sigh with relief but still feel apprehension. I'll have the same classmates in my fifth grade. Each and every one of them will be there. Though, who knows, maybe, just maybe, they'll leave me alone this year, and I'll be able to focus on studying well.

"I want to become an A student," I say dreamily.

Mom cocks her head. "How did you manage to get all Bs on your final exams if you skipped almost all the classes?"

"I figured out the answers on the go."

"Figured how?"

"I don't remember, just figured."

"But spelling . . ." Mom murmurs. "How did you do that?"

I think for a second, then remember what I did. "I sang the words out in my head."

Mom smiles proudly at me. "You don't say!"

"Do you want to hear about the circus now?" I ask, trying to distract her. I can't believe I've talked my way out of being punished. And it's good not to have secrets from Mom. For a year, I had to keep my teacher and everyone she sent from reaching our door and talking to Mom. Only one useful thing was developed in all that stress—thinking quickly on my feet.

"What circus?" Mom asks, settling back into her armchair.

"Didn't you know? Dad and I went to the circus today. The first thing we did was take a picture of me on a horse. It'll be ready in a few days."

Mom nods approvingly. "Victor always buys photographer's services when he has money."

Thanks to Dad, I even have a picture of me dressed in a Native American costume and wearing a long black wig. I also have a picture with a monkey and a picture with Grandpa and daffodils.

"When is Dad's birthday?" I ask.

"July 7, 1937," Mom answers.

"Lucky triple seven."

Do we celebrate Dad's birthdays? Do we celebrate mine or Mom's? I don't remember.

I look at my mother. She's knitting with the distant look I'm so used to.

"What's my year of birth?" I continue blabbering, probably because of all the stress.

"1983," she answers. "The year when the song 'Million Scarlet Roses' was released."

Alla Pugacheva is our favorite singer. She's the favorite singer of our entire neighborhood, city, and country. Her voice resembles Mom's, and I sometimes think the singer is our relative. Maybe Mom was listening to her songs while pregnant because I know all her lyrics by heart. Even my first memory of myself is from when I was a toddler, standing in the center of this room, holding a brush as a microphone and singing, "Alla, Alla Pugacheva." I think I couldn't yet speak well.

The tickets to Alla Pugacheva's concerts are scandalously expensive. Mom's friend who works at the Festival Concert Hall once smuggled us inside before a concert. We spent a day sitting in the electrical room and came out when the music started playing. Lucky us. We found two empty seats.

"Give me that pink ball of yarn," Mom says, pointing to the basket in the cabinet.

"And when is your birthday?" I ask, handing the yarn to her.

"March 26, 1959," she replies.

"But I saw in your passport that you were born in 1958."

Mom purses her lips in distaste and doesn't reply. Wait! Did she try to reduce her age? Does she think thirty-five years old is old, but thirty-four isn't? That's funny.

A knock on our window startles both of us, and we stiffen, staring at the window with wide eyes.

"Who's there?" Mom asks in a gruff voice, pretending to be a man.

"Daria," a voice on the other side answers uncertainly.

"Daria!" Mom exclaims, opening the curtain. "Are you OK?"

The young woman on the other side starts talking rapidly, "Yes, but I wanted to ask you to babysit. I was asked on a date."

I stare at her black pigtails in fascination. They're stuck out at uneven heights and bobbling as she continues to tell us excitedly that she wasn't expecting the offer and how much she wants to go.

"When do you need me?" Mom asks her.

"Right now," she answers sheepishly, tucking the escaped strands of her long bangs behind her ears.

"We'll be there," Mom says and smacks her lips.

"How old is her daughter?" I ask as Daria leaves, and Mom starts brushing her hair.

"Sophia is an infant."

"I adore small kids."

"Me too. Let's go."

We wash our hands and go outside, then up the driveway to the small stone house standing before the hundred-yard-wide strip of woods above.

The door of the house stands open. Daria calls for us to come in. She's probably seen us through a window.

The baby is sleeping soundly in her crib. I watch as if it's the most intriguing thing ever. I don't want to look at Daria, who's walking around in only a skirt and a bra while the iron is crackling nearby.

"Who's the lucky guy?" Mom asks her.

Daria laughs off the compliment, blushing.

"Answer, answer." Mom gently nudges her elbow.

"I tried to take the blinders off my eyes after my boyfriend left me," she says. "But here I am, trusting again. The guy is a TV repairman who came to my house and refused to take any money. The next thing I knew, I poured us tea, and we talked all evening long."

"Take men with a grain of salt," Mom says, pretending to be wise. She isn't.

"Yes, but, uh, I'm open to good things now."

"Soon, Sophia will be helping you."

I raise my eyebrows. Will she? I don't think I help Mom. Not at all.

"We'll take the baby for a walk and have her sleep in the fresh air," Mom says.

Daria helps her to lift Sophia out of the crib. "And I'll be back by 9 p.m. to breastfeed."

As we start walking down the street, we try to avoid the cars and their exhaust. We're heading for the sports stadium near school number eight.

When we get there, we sit in the bleachers, and Mom puts Sophia in my hands. "I'll run one lap on the track while you're sitting with her, then we'll change."

"Great idea," I say and wait for Mom to return.

We alternate a few times, and I enjoy both sitting with Sophia and running faster than the wind. The faster I am, the more time I get to spend with the baby.

Once again, I carefully take the bundle from Mom's hands and get in my seat. Sophia has just woken up and is all fidgety. I kiss her tiny fingers and tuck her arms back into the two sheets she's swaddled in.

"How are you, sweetie?" I ask and then tell her, "You're sweet as a puppy."

She looks at me quietly, her eyes unfocused and her lips puckered like pink marshmallows. Suddenly, the iron door to the nearby sports school opens, and a man dressed in blue workout attire steps on its terrace strip. I instinctively tug Sophia closer. The man smiles at me briefly, then focuses on Mom, who's finishing her lap.

As she comes to the stairs, he says to her, "I couldn't help but notice how beautiful your family is."

Mom rubs the back of her neck and nods but doesn't elaborate that the baby isn't ours. Cooing, she reaches for Sophia and cradles her to her chest.

I look through the open door inside the sports school. I can see a long row of training equipment. Fascinated by it, I try to figure out what is what.

"If you want to attend this gym, you're welcome," the man tells us, noticing my interest. "No payment is required."

My eyes widen at the offer. I'd love to come and train here, but does he really mean it? And what if he doesn't remember me when I come later? I'd be too shy to explain. And then there could be someone else asking me why I'm not paying.

"Let's go for a walk in Riviera Park," Mom tells me, stepping on the landing below.

I walk after her, and we head toward the gates, then across the river bridge and to the park's entrance. It's closed. Too late, alas.

"Where now?" I ask. "To the Singing Fountains maybe?"

Mom nods, then points her elbow at the magnolia trees. "Some of them still have flowers."

"They look like brides," I note. "I can climb and get some."

"No, they'll give us headaches. They're poisonous. We can buy an oil painting of them instead."

"We don't have enough money to buy necessities, let alone fancy art."

Mom looks away and changes the subject. "Listen, I forgot to tell you that the government has started hunting for stray dogs. We need to keep an eye on Mickey and Doll when they wander around."

"Why would the government do something so awful?" I ask incredulously.

"Stray dogs can be aggressive."

"I've never met one aggressive dog. Even dogs that bark guarding their houses wag their tails when I start talking to them in a sweet voice."

"Dog whisperer."

For the rest of the evening, we walk around the public garden, admire the full-blown flowers, and listen to the chirping of birds. The music of the Singing Fountains was too loud, so we didn't stay, just admired the colorful lights for a minute, then left.

After we return the baby to her happy mother, we go home. In Mom's and my room, I grab a pair of blue plastic hangers and start to skate on them. Our varnished parquet floor is perfectly slippery.

Fifteen minutes pass, and I get bored. Turning dramatically, I fall on my bed, pretending to have fainted. I wait and wait for Mom to run to me, screaming with worry, but she doesn't. I open one eye and watch her. Maybe she didn't see me fall? I stand up, sway back and forth, then repeat the "fainting." No reaction.

Frustrated, I get up and climb under my blanket. Images of the circus performances begin swirling in my mind. The animals, except the goats, were so smart. I wonder if rats are as smart.

I peek out from under the blanket and ask Mom, "How do the rats know not to bite us?"

"A rat once bit your step-grandpa's finger while he was asleep," she says.

"No way!" I say and duck my head back under the blanket. How will I be able to sleep now?

Poor Grandpa. Had he been scared? Probably not. I imagine that all the men with dark hair and dark eyes are very courageous and fearless, dark knights in shining armor. However, the only thing I remember about Grandpa's personality is he was funny, almost comical. We had lots of adventures together.

Once I fell into a utility hole and floated in its murky water while Grandpa was watching me with horror from above. I don't remember anything that happened after that—I must've lost my consciousness.

Another time, in the winter, he and I made a rock fortress at the beach and got splattered by an icy wave. We'd never run home faster than on that day, so eager to warm ourselves up with hot-water bottles and tea.

On and on, I remember all the other fun days Grandpa and I had. Hmm, I need to visit his grave soon.

Another Summer Day to Play

Awakened by the joyful squeals of kids outside our window, I open my eyes and strain my ears to hear better and enjoy the happiness in their voices. Now I wanna go to the courtyard and play too.

As I raise my head from the pillow, I see Mom sitting in a chair with Mickey wiggling in her lap.

"What happened?" I screech.

"He had an epileptic fit during the night," she explains, unwrapping Mickey from a fleece blanket. "I had to take him to a veterinarian."

I get up and walk to them, kneeling over our poor dog.

"Let him outside," Mom says. "He needs to use the bathroom."

"Sure." I open the doors for him and return to the room to get dressed.

"Do we have something to eat?" I ask.

Mom apologetically shakes her head, muttering, "I spent the last of my money on the veterinarian."

"It's OK. I'll find food."

I head for the courtyard, but the kids I heard earlier are nowhere to be seen. I turn and venture over the fence of one of our neighbors' gardens, slipping inside.

"Hi," a toddler shouts, proudly showing me his yellow swim ring.

"Hi," I reply and then smile.

As he and his mom continue on their way to the beach, I walk into the trees and jump up the trunk of the pear tree. I eat pears until my teeth hurt, then climb back down.

"I told you not to come to my garden," a woman shouts from one of the windows of the neighboring house.

Oops, I wasn't as quiet as I thought. I dart out of the garden and head back for my apartment, then knock on Dad's door.

"Hi, love," he says, opening it.

"Do you have a rope?" I ask.

He looks at me quizzically. "No, for what?"

"I wanted to make a tree swing."

"I have fishing lines you can braid into a rope."

"Great, give them to me."

While I wait for Dad in the doorway, I scan his room. Judging by the chunks of wood and sawdust scattered around the floor, he's been making furniture for a neighbor's order. The room looks like a workshop. We're going to get some money soon.

Dad returns from the balcony with a bunch of super-long, evenly-cut fishing lines. I curtsy as thanks and run outside.

It's a good day to be in the fresh air. The courtyard is still empty. I shrug to myself and go to the oak tree beside Dad's garden. When I reach it, I sling the lines over my shoulder and climb up to the sturdiest-looking branch. I roll the lines around it a few times and finish it with a triple knot. Perfect.

As I start climbing down, something makes me glance up at our apartment building. In one of the open windows, I see a family of seven sitting at the dining table, chatting and eating in the coziness of their well-lit kitchen.

I feel a sudden pang of envy. *How would it feel to have a typical family?*

"Hey, are you a rock climber?" a boy shouts from the courtyard.

Do I know him? From school? Mentally, I put a dark school uniform with a red scarf on him. Nope, he's just a passerby.

I raise my chin proudly and nod, then climb up higher just to show him how much farther I can go. *A rock climber, yeah.* It was a miracle I didn't fall from the cherry tree yesterday.

After making sure the boy has gone, I climb down, then go to Dad's garden and search for a thick stick. There are many of them because Dad recently trimmed some big trees for our neighbors. I grab one such stick and return to the oak tree.

After tying it and the lines together, I raise my knee and settle onto my perfect swing seat.

"Laura," Ava shouts from her window, her wheat-colored hair spiking in all directions like there was an explosion in a macaroni factory.

"Come outside!" I yell to her. "See what I've made."

"I'm waiting for everyone to return home."

"Oh, that's a pity."

Ava disappears from her window, and I clutch the lines tightly with my hand, take a few steps back, and push myself up into the air. The exhilaration is instant. I'm flying. But before I can even squeal with joy, there's a snap above me, and I feel myself falling onto the rosebushes below. Boom!

If only I'd braided the fishing lines like Dad told me. Here I am, lying in the thorns, covered with the lines like they're cobwebs. I have difficulty breathing from the hit to my back. It's like I've choked on a piece of bread. The tickling in my back stops, and I raise my head.

I hope my neighbors didn't see me fall, otherwise they'd call for an ambulance like they did when they saw me fall from a handrail.

Being careful, I untangle myself from the lines and branches, then scramble out onto the soft grass beside the bush. My forearms and legs are scraped; little droplets of blood trickle around the cuts. I need to find some Plantago leaves to put on the scratches. They'll stop the blood and help with healing.

The last time I used Plantago leaves was when an angry rooster attacked me. It flew out of nowhere, grabbed my arm with its sharp claws, and wouldn't let go. I had to run to the courthouse's fountain and dive in. It sounds funny now, but at the time I felt hurt.

In the cracks in the cement courtyard, I find plenty of Plantago and rip the widest leaves, plastering them on my arms and legs. I give it time for it to work its magic, then go to another of my neighbors' gardens. Time to eat again.

I see some redcurrants growing in the minty-smelling grass and launch myself at them. Usually, like blackberries, they only grow at the start of summer, so I'm very lucky to find them in mid-August.

After I eat them, I run to the apartment building and start knocking on my friends' doors. It's so boring to be alone with my uninteresting thoughts. I'd rather be asleep than tortured by them.

The first girl to agree to come out is a tourist from Vladivostok. I heard it took her family ten days and two trains to travel across all Russia just to visit Sochi and swim in the Black Sea. Isn't that wacky?

"I'll tell Mom and be out in a minute," she tells me.

I wait for her at the door, and when she returns, we go to the courtyard.

"I forgot your name," I mumble.

"Marina," she says, and cute hollows appear on her cheeks as she smiles. "How old are you?"

I decide to lie. "I'm twelve years old."

"Wow, I'm only eight."

Suddenly, an idea comes to me. Why not have a little more fun?

"You know, Marina," I start, "I can read people's thoughts just by looking into their eyes."

"How so?" she gasps.

"Magical powers."

As I expected, Marina is impressed, her brilliant blue eyes wide as saucers. But as the wind blows her blond hair in different directions, I think that if someone here were a witch, it would be her.

"So," I begin, "the magical powers came to me after a near-death experience."

"Cooool," Marina drawls. "What happened?"

"I fell down the stairs."

Marina draws in her breath sharply and asks, "So what am I thinking right now?"

"Umm . . . I only can detect if you're telling the truth or not. Kind of 'yes' or 'no' answers."

"Interesting. I want to go to your apartment and play with your toys. Am I telling the truth?"

I bend and stare into her eyes. "You . . . are . . . telling . . . the truth."

I grab her hand and lead her to my apartment. "Let's go. I have a small baby doll that looks just like you—blond with blue eyes."

We walk into Mom's and my room. I open my small cabinet full of toys, and we start playing while Marina keeps testing my "abilities" to distinguish the truth from lies. I'm pretty sure I get every answer correct.

"My mom only allowed me twenty minutes," Marina says, getting up from the floor.

"Go ask your mom for fifteen additional minutes," I suggest.

She lowers her eyes sheepishly. "She has a doctor's appointment, and I need to go with her."

"But you're tourists in Sochi."

"Yeah, but Mom got worms from eating strawberries," she says, then adds conspiratorially, "Long like spaghetti."

I jump to my feet. "You can go now."

She snickers, then tiptoes playfully out of the room. I wait to hear the front door closing, then rush to the kitchen sink and wash my hands with soap three times.

Returning to the room, I stuff the toys back into the cabinet and stare at them. Something doesn't seem right. I count and count. One is missing. To my utter shock, it's the small blond doll. I check and recheck. It's not here. *One liar duped the other.*

I go knocking on Marina's front door. No answer. I bang again and again. Marina and her mother have apparently already left. I sigh heavily and go knock on my other friends' doors. It seems everyone's at the beach today. What should I do now? *Go to Grandpa's grave.*

Happy that I now have a purpose, I dash to the street stairs and jog down the hill toward the bus stop. From the corner of my eye, I see my mother walking in the opposite direction, not seeing me at all, too engrossed in piercing her nails with a sewing needle. She passes right by me like a zombie, doing that horrible thing for everyone to see.

I bite my lip painfully and continue on my way to the bus stop. Bus number twenty-six is coming along, and I hold up my hand to signal the driver to stop. He does. I gratefully smile at him and sit in my favorite seat at the back. The window here is rolled down, and I can enjoy the breeze.

I shift forward and blow on the closed window ahead of me, then quickly write my name in the fog.

"Girl, don't touch the window with your lips," one of the passengers tells me. "Sick people leave their germs there."

I turn and look at the man who spoke. It doesn't seem he's very afraid of germs himself. There's dirt under his nails. Still, I appreciate his care. He's not like some weirdos I meet sometimes on the bus. Once a man tried to press his body into me, and I stepped on his foot forcefully so he'd keep his distance.

The bus is passing school number fourteen now. It means that the cemetery is the next stop. I get up and squeeze between the passengers, then stand at the rear door, waiting. As it opens, I hop out and run to the entrance trail.

Grandpa's small grave is a short distance away. I walk through the trees and bushes and recognize Grandpa's name on one of the tombstones, almost buried under tall weeds. The grave's flower bed is supposed to have . . . well, flowers, but instead, it has these. I try to tug them out, but the roots are too strong for my hands.

I sit down on the edge of the grave and silently recite the prayers I know. It's so relaxing to be here, listening to the birds chirping through the silence. Sometimes, though, they shriek like lost spirits, and it's spooky.

I also like reading what's engraved on the other headstones and sculptures and poring over the photographs of people who lived before. I only don't like seeing the graves of kids. It makes me sad.

The cemetery has another dark side. I recently heard that a madman in a mask was lurking there, howling like a wounded wolf, kneeling and rocking at the different graves. A shudder of fear runs through me. I'd better leave.

Bye, Grandpa. I get up and look at the metal tables next to some of the graves. Sometimes the relatives of the dead leave candies there, believing the spirits will eat the offerings. I know it's just an old wives' tale, so I wouldn't mind grabbing some for myself. But there are none today.

I dust off the leaves from my bottom and scurry back to the bus stop. Again, I catch bus number twenty-six and ride it as it circles the city and brings me back to the bus stop near my home.

Back in my courtyard, I sit on the bench packed with older ladies from our neighborhood and listen to them talk. I have a reserved place on the bench, on its right edge. My friends laugh at me for liking to hang out with older ladies. I can just imagine what they see—me, with my tangled, unevenly cut hair, and the older ladies, with their colorful floral headscarves.

"How have you been?" Mrs. Dub asks, squinting her eyes with their long white lashes at me.

All eleven ladies on the bench cock their heads, waiting for my answer.

"I've been good," I reply. "Just visited my grandfather's grave."

Everyone sighs their approval.

"What a wonderful granddaughter!" Mrs. Zorina exclaims.

I beam at her. She usually looks exhausted but not today. Even her deep wrinkles seem smoother somehow.

"Theodor wasn't even her biological grandfather," Mrs. Guseva remarks to no one in particular, cooling herself with a pink fan.

I look at the small pictures plastered on it. Big Russian cities, I think.

Another neighbor, Mrs. Lis, says, "Theodor was the only one who kept an eye on Laura."

"We all watched over Laura," contradicts my next-door neighbor Mrs. Yermol, buttoning up her purple dress with her oily hands. Not really oily, but they often seem to be glistening. Maybe because she cooks so much.

Mrs. Lis looks startled by the strength in Mrs. Yermol's voice, and she relents. "Yes, you're right."

Involuntarily, my gaze slides to Mrs. Lis's big stomach. Why is it so big? She starts laughing.

"I've had a big stomach since I was in my forties," she explains, guessing my thoughts. "People on the bus were giving up their seats to me, assuming I was pregnant."

We all laugh, then the ladies start discussing the sappy *Santa Barbara* soap opera that's currently on TV. I tune out. That show isn't my thing. *The Rich Also Cry* and *Simple Maria* are. When Mrs. Yermol isn't renting her spare room to tourists, I go to her place, and we watch a new episode each evening. I even chose my name, Laura, when I heard it on *Simple Maria*. The letters in the name sounded magical, and I saw its aura as light green with yellow.

Before that, my name was Alexandra. I never liked it—not because it wasn't pretty (it was)—but because it had derivatives that were used mainly by boys: Sasha, Shura, and Sanya. I wanted a girly-girl name.

A lady from the house next to ours asks me if I scratched myself. I don't remember her name, but I recognize her villagey accent with the overstressed letter *o*'s that we normally pronounce as schwa.

I look at my knees and at the scratches. "Yes, I fell."

"As the Russian saying puts it, 'All your wounds will heal by the time of your wedding,'" she says, cackling.

Wedding? I shake my head. I'll probably never have a wedding. Who would want to marry me?

"I better go and make dinner for my husband," the lady with the accent says, struggling to a standing position. "Or he'll yell at me again for not doing my chores."

The remaining ten ladies look at her sympathetically, then watch her amble up the driveway and to the adjacent house on the right. I must say, her peacock-feather-green dress looks quite elegant in spite of the fact the older ladies always wear the clothes from their youth—at least that's what Mrs. Yermol told me.

"Did you see the comedian Zadornov on TV?" Mrs. Bykova asks the other ladies. "He said people in America were stupid and told funny stories about them."

She sounds grouchy. I'm not surprised, though. Mrs. Bykova always used to shout at us kids for one thing or another, especially for being noisy. As if it's possible to keep it down while playing. Now that she has to use crutches to walk, she mainly leaves us alone.

Mrs. Zayka, my almost next-door neighbor, shakes her head disapprovingly. "A group of Americans came recently to my grandson's school. They were very nice. Not stupid at all."

Her green eyes are so expressive. Who would dare argue with this small woman with a big heart?

The ladies change the topic again, but I continue thinking of the name America. It sounds so cool. Now I'd like to have it as my surname. My friends and classmates would be so jealous. Kids, not like the older ladies, know that America is a great country because it's the home of Disney World.

From the apartment building emerges a very pretty teenage girl. All ten ladies turn their heads to gawk at her. The girl politely says hello and continues on her way up the driveway, carefully watching her steps. She has on some big sandals that look like little black tanks.

"Just look at her," Mrs. Maslina whispers, rattling a set of keys in her knobby fingers. The noise is bugging me, and I look at the keys as if they're my enemies.

"What a shame she's dressed in such a short skirt," says a cousin of Mrs. Zayka's. "In Georgia and Abkhazia, we were never allowed to dress like that."

I turn to look at her. She's dressed neatly in a long-sleeved black dress that covers even her wrists. Unsuitable for summer but somehow stylish.

"Her heavy makeup is horrible," Mrs. Bykova barks, and almost everyone murmurs agreement.

"Why didn't her older brother forbid her from dressing like a . . . like that?" Mrs. Guseva grumbles.

"And where did she get the money to buy those expensive platform shoes?" Mrs. Yermol asks rhetorically. "Her family is poor."

"Mm-hmm," Mrs. Blinova grunts in agreement. Wait! How could she see? She's supposed to be visually impaired after she suffered a stroke last year. Her enormous green eyes just stare ahead, unfocused.

As the older ladies continue to share their opinions, I add mine too. "Maybe she just wants to look like a Barbie doll, and that's why she wears the beautiful short skirt."

My neighbors seem to mull it over for a few seconds, and I smile with a tinge of satisfaction at defending the girl.

"Can I ask someone for a cup of sugar?" I ask, getting to my feet.

"Of course," Mrs. Yermol replies. "Now?"

"Now. I want sweet tea very much."

I help Mrs. Yermol to her feet, and we walk along the narrow pathway leading to our porch.

"I'll also warm you some soup," Mrs. Yermol says.

"Yum-yum," I say. "Do you remember the time when we could only buy one kilogram of sugar a month?"

"Of course, what with the food shortages after the collapse of the USSR."

I nod. "I was finishing my sugar so fast that I blamed Mom for stealing it. I feel ashamed now."

"Apologize," Mrs. Yermol suggests simply.

I shrug, and we continue along the entrance hall in silence. When we enter her apartment, we head for the kitchen, and she makes good on her promise and warms the soup for me. I gulp it in less than a minute.

"Delicious," I comment, wiping my mouth with the napkin Mrs. Yermol offers.

"You forgot to say thank you," she admonishes.

I hesitate. When will I get used to niceties? They feel so fake to me. I say thank you sometimes when I really, really mean it or if I don't know the person well, so it's easier.

I force myself to say it this time but super quietly. "Thank you."

Mrs. Yermol hands me a plastic bag filled with sugar, laughing. "I remember how we old ladies were teaching you to say thank you over and over again. You were refusing to, even for candies.

"Cat got my tongue," I quip, exiting her apartment and walking across the entrance hall toward my door.

"Proper manners are important. We also taught you a bunch of new words because you didn't have a good vocabulary, even when you were three."

"I only remember you teaching me how to write by hand."

"That too. I worked as a teacher all my life, and I love to teach."

"Interesting. I also want to become a teacher."

She chuckles kindly. "I hope you'll succeed. Oh, I've remembered something I wanted to ask. Is it true that you had a fight with that boy Arthur?"

"Not a fight. We just tested if boys were really stronger than girls."

"And were they?"

"They were," I reply and giggle.

Mrs. Yermol pats me on the head and moves on down the entrance hall. I open my front door and go light up the gas stove to boil some water for my tea. I can have as much sugar as I want today. Let it be four teaspoons a cup. Hmm . . . I suddenly remember my mother's friend Luisa, who was horrified when she saw how much sugar I ate. She scolded me until I cried, but Mom took my side. Secretly, though, I know Luisa was right.

I drink four cups of tea and try not to think of how much sugar I've consumed. Happy and satisfied, I run back into the courtyard and sit back on the bench with the ladies.

My timing is perfect. Kristen and her mom are walking down our hilly driveway. They're obviously returning from the beach—Kristen's braids are wet, her skin tanned. My skin only burns, turning an angry red. I heard that a rare nut oil can help you get a brown tan. Next summer, I'll search for it in the stores around the city.

"Stay and play with me!" I yell to Kristen as she gets closer.

"Allow her twenty minutes to dine," her mom says sternly.

I cringe a little at her tone. I forgot how uneasy Kristen's mom makes me. She never understands jokes and often interprets things wrong. Once when I told her how beautiful she looked that day, she got offended, thinking I meant she was ugly on all the other days.

As Kristen and her mom disappear from view, I get up and walk in circles around the yard, then go along the pathway around the building and chew on grape tendrils growing from the neighbors' windows.

The upper parts of rose stems are much more delicious, and I walk over to the rosebushes. My favorite plant, though, is honeysuckle, but it's not blooming now.

I raise my head and spot the twin sisters Natalie and Angelina in their kitchen window. They're seventeen years old and look just like Barbie dolls, except their hair isn't such a bright blond color.

I run toward their window and climb onto the ledge of the building. I've missed these sisters. They travel to Sochi only in summers to visit their grandparents and swim in the sea.

"Natalie! Angelina!" I squeal with delight.

I can tell them apart because Natalie seems thinner.

"Wow, you've grown so much!" Angelina exclaims, smiling.

"Not a cutie anymore," Natalie jokes.

I look at her, my feelings wounded, but shrug nonchalantly. "Kristen is still a cutie."

"I bet," Natalie says.

I peer inside their window. A piece of an omelet with bologna is sitting on the table, looking yummy. I tear my gaze away guiltily and raise it back to the sisters.

"What were you doing all day?" I ask them.

"Studying English," Natalie replies. "And now we're resting our eyes by looking at the green leaves."

"Does it help?"

"Yes, especially if you blink for a minute and then stare into the distance."

I nod and then lie, "I know English."

"Say something to us then," Natalie and Angelina ask together.

Now what? I can imitate the words from the English songs I've heard at the beach and say some words Mom taught me.

"*Goodbye*," I say in English and jump off the wall to the ground so they can't ask me for more English words. "I need to hurry."

"That's amazing!" yells Natalie. "She truly speaks it."

As an afterthought, I ask in Russian, "Do you still share a boyfriend between the two of you?"

"Quiet," Natalie hisses. "Grandma can hear you."

"Will you take me with you again when you go on a date?" I whisper.

"Absolutely not," Natalie answers indignantly.

"Will you take me to the beach with you, then?"

"Yes, and we'll buy you an ice cream."

"I can't wait for that."

I turn and skip back to the courtyard, happy as a dog with two tails. Ice cream! Yes, please.

Uh-oh. Kristen is already in the courtyard, waiting for me and tapping her foot impatiently.

"I thought you'd be here," she says when she sees me.

"Sorry," I say. "Let's play now."

"Play what?" she asks with an attitude.

"Let's sell something again. Bouquets of flowers?"

"Where will we get them?"

"Make them ourselves, duh." I gesture at all the flowers growing around our courtyard, and Kristen gives me a thumbs-up.

"Do you have thread at your house?" I ask. "We'll need it to tie the flowers together."

"Yes, I'll go ask Mom," she says, hurrying toward the stairs to her porch.

I look around again at the surrounding gardens. I'll pick pink roses and green hydrangeas. For my second bouquet, I'll get hibiscuses. Oh, and later we can play royal dolls with them.

"Let's start," Kristen whoops, returning to the courtyard.

We begin our work, and Kristen's bouquets turn out to be much more presentable than mine. She uses lots of foliage and plants I'd have never thought of as decoration. She has an artistic gene, for sure. Without a doubt, we can sell her bouquets faster.

I bite off long threads from the spool and help Kristen tie them over her bouquets. Following this, I bite off another, even longer thread and go tie it between two trees at the entrance to our courtyard. Passersby will have to purchase our merchandise if they want to go through this shortcut to get to their street.

"Sit there," I tell Kristen, pointing to the side opposite me.

"A woman is coming up," she whispers.

I turn and see a young woman walking up the street stairs, with her hair teased into a crown. *Good, she looks wealthy.*

Plastering a big smile on my face, I wait for her to finish the climb, then say, "To go through our courtyard, you'll need to buy a bouquet."

"Choose the one that looks at you better," Kristen adds.

Looks at you? I try not to laugh.

The woman doesn't stop, however. She keeps moving forward like a bulldozer, tearing our thread with her hips. My eyes bulge out in disbelief. What a harpy! To make matters worse, she huffs at us with annoyance.

"We'll get the next one," Kristen tells me, positive as ever.

"Hey, girls, what's up?" my dad asks, coming out of the building.

Kristen lifts our four bouquets over her head. "We're selling flowers."

"For how much?"

Kristen looks at me for the answer, as always.

"One hundred rubles?" I reply, but it comes out as a question. This sum should be enough to buy two simple ice creams called Plombir.

"Can I get a discount?" Dad asks. "I can buy all the bouquets for three hundred rubles."

"Deal," Kristen and I shout simultaneously and start jumping.

Bad Business

The next morning I wake up feeling like I slept well. I look around and see that Mom has finally left for work on time.

I stay in bed and listen through the ceiling to the voices of Ava and her older brother, George, playing upstairs. Does Ava know how fortunate she is to have an older brother? He always protects her. Some people are just born lucky. Not me—I'm a magnet for trouble.

I slide out of bed and wander over to our double-door wardrobe. One side is for my things, the other for Mom's. I dig through the crumpled materials of my clothes—not really mine; almost all of them are hand-me-downs—and choose an outfit that will probably be tight because my friends who gave it to me are smaller. Red pants and a silky blue blouse. Glamorous!

I tug my nightgown over my head and toss it into the wardrobe, then bend my knee to slide my leg into the pants. Something makes me glance up, and I lock eyes with a bearded man standing on the other side of my window, staring at me. My heart lurches, and I squeak in horror, jumping back. *Panic.*

"Don't be shy, sweetheart," he murmurs, looking me up and down with his beady eyes. Pinocchio's Stromboli that wants to swallow me up.

"Dad!" I scream.

Dad doesn't come—he probably isn't home—but it's enough to scare the pervert into running away. I dash to the window and close the curtains. I hope all the bearded men I meet in the future won't be associated in my mind with Peeping Toms.

I finish dressing, button the blouse up, and go to the kitchen, where I eat the last piece of a flounder fish I bought yesterday. After washing it down with tea, I go out into the courtyard.

No one's here so early, not even the lady neighbors. I leave the place and go to the trade gallery district to do some window shopping. With my cool outfit, people will think I'm rich. Next time, I can stuff cotton into an empty Mars candy bar wrapper and pour water mixed with a touch of orange paint into an empty Fanta bottle. If I were carrying those two things, people would think I'm rich indeed.

The first store I come to is Kids' World, a place where families buy toys for their kids. It also has school supplies and clothes. A place out of a fairy tale . . . if you have money, of course.

I approach the oversized store entrance, look through its floor-to-ceiling glass, and step inside. The counters are long and endless, all covered in toys. The most expensive things are displayed on shelves on the wall or in separate cabinets.

At the end of the toy department's vast hall stands the most luxurious curio cabinet, shining like a huge diamond. Inside are the toys I want most of all in life—Barbie dolls. I close my eyes and try to imagine a Barbie doll in my hands. My skin tingles. I open my eyes again and stare at the cabinet. Row after row of gorgeous dolls sparkling in their silky gowns and lacy bows. Reverently, I walk closer to the cabinet and read the sign: "Don't touch the glass."

I bite my lip. If only I could buy one of them. Each girl in my neighborhood has a Barbie doll but not me. Would I choose the doll in the white dress or the pink? Or the blue? Pink and white make me feel happy.

I turn away and try not to torture myself anymore. I see at least five shop assistants standing behind the counters of different sections. They're all dressed in long, gray uniform dresses. One shop assistant with blond, bouncy curls has four customers gathered around her. They're talking.

"All toys are made in Russia," the shop assistant says.

I go closer and look at the shelf with stuffed animals. There are bunches of teddy bears, soft bunnies, and fluffy kittens.

"Could you show me that pink bear, please?" a customer wearing gumball earrings asks.

The shop assistant immediately rises on her tiptoes and gets the bear. I lean on the counter and stare at the toy too. After turning it in her hands a few times, the customer loses interest, places it on the counter, and turns to look at the other stuffed animals.

The teddy bear is now lying alone, with its cute nose and adorably fuzzy ears sticking out. It's been completely forgotten by the shop assistant, who's busy again, cheerfully chatting with a bunch of new customers.

I blink a few times, unable to process my sudden urge. Should I take the toy? With a heavy conscience, I make a split-second decision to do so. I lift the bear from the counter and dart to the exit.

In the thick of the crowd, I continue running up the trade gallery alley. After I make sure no one's following me, I stop and sit down on the cool stairs of an electronics store. *Why did I do that?* I don't need any toy animals when I have real ones.

But . . . what if . . . ? I stand up and hurry back to the store. At the entrance, I hesitate for a second, then step inside. The place is still crowded. No one will recognize me, surely. Just in case, though, I edge away from the view of the blond shop assistant and quickly walk to one of the cashier booths.

"Ma'am, my parents scolded me for buying this teddy bear," I say to the woman behind the plastic wall. "Could I make a return?"

"Of course, dear," she says kindly and gets up. "I'll refund this. No problem."

"Thank you," I say, remembering Mrs. Yermol's teachings.

"I just need to ask the shop assistants how much it costs. I'll be right back."

I bend my knees and slowly disappear under the blue panels of the booth. When the cashier returns, I smile at her gratefully.

I take a moment to admire her heart-shaped face and thick eyelashes, then my gaze falls to the open register drawer as the woman counts out a few bills. Uff, I feel so guilty. Maybe I just need to let it go and leave before she gives me the money?

Food. The thought makes me lift my hand and reach for the money.

"Thank you," I say again to this kind lady. *And forgive me, please.*

I head to the grocery store and walk inside. Making circles, I try to choose what I want most. Sunflower-seed brittle, halvah, potato chips, and Buratino soda. I add up the prices and determine there's just enough money. I go pay the total and return to the counter with the receipt for proof. The shop assistant gives me my treats, and I march happily outside.

I stroll along the trade gallery alley in the other direction from the toy store and eat the brittle. I stop to uncork the bottle of soda on the edge of a concrete planter, then continue on my way. I bounce my knees to the music playing from some store nearby, not understanding how others are able to walk out of rhythm.

I examine the long supporting wall adorned with a never-ending mosaic of small and colorful pieces of tile, creating enormous figures that were obviously inspired by cartoon characters. I can't imagine how much patience the workers had to make it all by hand.

At the end of the path, I turn and go back, then cross the road toward the government administration building. The small path takes me to Flag Square, where a woman is sitting on the ground, barefoot, with an infant in her lap. A beggar. My face falls—I must give away the potato chips and halvah I still have. The poverty-stricken woman needs it more.

I go closer and place my remaining snacks at the hem of her white dress. I look up, expecting gratitude but see only confusion. She keeps eyeing the packs with an odd expression on her face. Isn't she happy to have the food? I put the empty bottle on the ground too. She can sell it at the recycling center later.

I leave her alone to her thoughts and go across Parkovaya Street. My own thoughts turn into worries and fears. Will God forgive me for stealing? I vividly remember an older man who showed me his two net bags dripping with kefir. He told me he stole two glass bottles of it from a store, and God punished him by making him fall. I felt sorry for the man, and now I have a premonition that I'm also going to be punished. To cut my bothersome thoughts off and escape them, I start running full speed.

In the courtyard, I find that there's still no one around, but I can hear girls' voices coming from the backyard. I round the building, following the sounds, and find Ava and three other girls I don't know taking turns playing a handheld Tetris game.

"These are my classmates," Ava says when she sees me. "Larisa, Diana, and Kira."

"I'm Laura," I say to them and step next to Ava, suddenly feeling self-conscious.

The girls continue playing, and I gingerly inch closer to them, watching the screen over their shoulders. They make so many mistakes when it seems so easy.

"Whose Tetris is this?" I ask, hoping it's Ava's because then I can ask her to lend it to me for a day.

"Mine," answers one of the girls, revealing her missing front teeth. Kira or Diana? I feel embarrassed to ask for their names again.

"I'm tired of sitting for so long," Ava says, getting up from the curb. "Let's play ballet."

For the following half an hour, we jump splits in the air and pretend to sing opera. Afterward, Larisa, who's wearing a white patch over her eye, teaches us how to play the hand game Rock, Paper, Scissors. I try to find out what happened to her eye, but each time I ask, she avoids the question.

Next, we recite funny rhymes we remember by heart, and then we decide to play the game Sea, Figure, Freeze. This game is all about movements. I can pantomime any character I choose, laugh when no one can guess who I am, and dramatically freeze when they press my imaginary stop button.

Before we can start the game, though, Ava's mom appears on their balcony, calling for her and the guests to come upstairs for dinner. Ava's mom's beauty is striking. She has black hair and dark blue eyes. I've never seen this combination on anyone else.

"OK," Ava replies and turns to smile at me apologetically. "Maybe we'll come back down in an hour."

Only a few minutes later, the girls disappear up the stairs, and I stay in the backyard alone, feeling disappointed. In full silence, I start hearing Mom's and Dad's voices coming out our back windows.

"Die, dickhead!" *Mom's voice.*

"After you, cunt!" *Dad's.*

I pretend I don't hear them and go to the meadow behind the backyard, where wild cats disguise themselves in the shrubbery. They hiss at me, and I give them space, walking around and practicing whistling with my lips pursed. I can only whistle by sucking air in, not blowing it out.

What to do next? Maybe I can go to Mrs. Yermol's apartment. I stand, rush up to the short flight of stairs, run to Mrs. Yermol's door, and ring the bell.

Ugh, I can hear my parents' voices again.

"Bastard!" Mom shouts.

"Whore!" Dad returns.

This is ridiculous—Mom is no whore.

"Faggot!" Mom yells.

What's a faggot?

Finally, Mrs. Yermol's door opens, and I leap inside, ending my torture.

"Sorry," she says. "I was cooking, and my hands were sticky."

"Can I help you cook?" I ask.

"Sure, but wash your hands first."

I kick off my flip-flops, go to the kitchen sink, and twist both faucets on.

"I was just thinking of you earlier," Mrs. Yermol says.

"Oh?" I ask.

"I was hoping you'd go to the grocery store to buy me bread and foie gras."

"Now?"

"Not now. You can do it in the evening."

The Mayak radio station is blasting from a plastic box on the wall, telling the time in Moscow, then talking about President Yeltsin. I sit down at the table and draw letters on its floured surface with my finger.

In two minutes Mrs. Yermol dumps more flour on the table, forms a little mountain with her hands, then says, "Dig a well in its center."

I carefully spiral my fingers through the middle, and Mrs. Yermol breaks an egg into the formed hole. Then she adds the other ingredients and starts kneading the mass with the heels of her hands for ten minutes. What a laborious job!

"This seems too hard," I note.

"I spent all day yesterday whisking egg whites with a tablespoon," she says.

"Why would you do that?"

"To make frosting for cupcakes. Do you like them? Do you want one?"

"Yes."

"Open the fridge and help yourself."

I eagerly do as I'm told, lifting one cupcake from the container and biting in. Mmm. The white frosting has a distinct lemony taste. De-licious.

"What is it going to become?" I ask, returning to the table.

"Pastries with strawberry preserves," Mrs. Yermol answers, brushing her hand against her short hair, unknowingly dusting it with flour.

"Sounds yummy."

"What were you up to today?"

I ignore the question and decide to tell a story from another day instead. "Once, in a bakery shop, I stared at a doughnut for so long that the saleswoman there gave it to me for free, just to get rid of me."

Mrs. Yermol laughs good-naturedly. "You're too big to use this trick anymore."

"I guess . . . When will you start baking the pastries?"

"The dough needs to rise overnight first."

"I can go and buy your groceries then."

"Thank you, dear. You're the only one I trust with money."

I remove the bits of dough from under my nails, wash my hands a third time, and take the bills. I decide to go to the store at the seaport. Somehow I don't feel right going to the grocery store I was in earlier.

It takes me no time to choose the necessary groceries, pay for them, and bring the bag and the change to Mrs. Yermol, who's now seated in the courtyard with her lady friends.

At home, everything is quiet; my parents probably got tired of shouting and are relaxing now. I knock on Mom's and my door. When she opens it, she hugs me to her, then steps back and squeezes my cheeks with her hands, kissing them one at a time. I laugh, amazed at how quickly Mom can spring back to normal after her and Dad's fights, looking cheerful and behaving like nothing happened. Is she that used to it?

I change into my home dress and toss my outfit onto the upper shelf. Should I iron my clothes? No, I usually end up burning my hands. I shudder at memories of the times I burned myself. Involuntarily, I also remember some other times I got burned. Once I stuck an electric plug with its cord cut off into a wall outlet, and it exploded. My fingertips turned purple. Another time, I leaned on the scorching bulb of a wall lamp, and my skin became all bubbly.

No, no ironing for me. I crawl into bed and watch Mom as she almost magically produces a sweater, layer by layer. My eyes grow heavy. The metal clicking of the knitting needles gets farther and farther away. *Click-clack, click-clack . . .*

It's well into the night when I wake up from the sound of the downpour drumming on the roofs, walls, and ground outside. The puddles are sloshing, giving me a sweet, happy feeling. Lifting my blanket, I get out of my bed and tiptoe to Mom's. I lie down next to her and press my face into her warm, almost hot, back. *Sweet.*

Chapter Six
Father's Wisdom

"Barbie." This word spins in my brain when I wake up. Have I been dreaming of her? I should start earning money for the doll of my dreams today.

As is my habit, I look around for Mom. She's gone to work. Why would she do that in such bad weather? It's still raining. The tea bushes will be wet and muddy. Mom won't be able to hold an umbrella while harvesting the leaves with one hand and holding a long bag with the other.

As the thunder booms, I tumble onto the floor, startled, then squeeze my eyes as the lightning strikes. It could kill my mother. She's in an open field. I begin to cry.

The next thunder comes, and I slide to the window and start to pray through my hiccups. The storm seems to last forever. I beg and beg God to stop it. He finally does.

I rise from my knees and go to the bathroom to wash my face. I can think of a Barbie doll again. I'll need to get at least 4,000 rubles. But how? Where? The unbidden thought comes—*in the toy store.*

My conscience tries to argue with me, to talk me out of this bad thing. It's a sin, and I heard that there's karma that would boomerang everything back.

I sit on my bed for ten minutes, reciting all the reasons why stealing is a horrible, horrible thing, but in the end, my good conscience loses its battle with my bad one.

I get up, slide into my comfortable yellow shoes, and run outside. God will punish me, for sure. What if I pretend just for one day that I don't believe in him? No God, no punishment. Can it work this way?

The fresh air is slightly cool after the rain, so I start running even faster to warm myself up. At the store's entrance, I stop and look through the glass walls to see if I recognize anyone from yesterday. Nope. Forcing a deep breath for courage, I casually stroll in and head for the familiar shelves.

For a moment, I pause to glance at the section of the toy department where marionettes are on display. I once threw a tantrum in front of my mother, begging her to buy me one of them, knowing very well she didn't have the money. Maybe I can ask the shop assistant for one of those marionettes? No, the purpose of earning money is to start collecting it for a Barbie doll. I look at the Barbie cabinet. It's outside the counter area, so I won't be able to ask straight for her.

I edge closer to the counter with the familiar teddy bears. The new shop assistant is older than the one from yesterday and doesn't look as cheery. Even her emerald necklace doesn't add any light to her eyes. Is this why customers aren't gathered around her? No one's here to shield me.

"Ma'am," I address her, "could you please show me that pink teddy bear?"

She fetches the toy, and I take it from her hands, then stare at the woman. *Turn away.* She doesn't. I feel my nose itching with nerves. What should I do now?

Clutching the teddy bear tightly, I look left and right, then bolt to the exit, ignoring the woman's shouts.

Outside, I keep running. I pass the city's main pharmacy, the central optical store, the cinnamon roll café, and Mom's favorite technology store, Zenith. I stop and lean on one of the long columns to think. I can't go back to the toy store, as everyone got a good look at me. As a matter of fact, I'll never be able to go to Kids' World again. I've really screwed up.

Now what to do with this teddy bear? If I keep it, it'll remind me every day that I'm a bad girl. It'd be better to give it to Kristen or Ava. Or . . . what if I ask other stores selling similar teddy bears to give me a refund? *Great idea.*

"Hey, you, don't move!" a voice shouts from behind.

I freeze, then slowly turn my head. As if in a nightmarish dream, I see the shop assistant. *Oh no!*

Huffing and puffing, she quickly approaches me and yanks the teddy bear from my hand.

"Come on," she growls, pinning me with her furious gaze.

She squeezes my hand and drags me back into the store.

"This girl is a thief!" she declares to all the customers.

I stand under their scrutiny for a long, miserable moment. Today must be the most humiliating day of my life.

"What's your name?" the shop assistant demands, letting go of my hand and folding her arms across her chest.

"L-L-Laura," I stutter. It's very difficult to breathe. I open my mouth and inhale sharply.

"Where do you live?"

I turn and point to the apartment building visible through the glass walls. "There."

"What's the number of your apartment?"

"Nine."

"And your school?" It feels like she's shooting these questions at me.

"Two."

My upper lip starts to tremble. I'm going to cry now. How could I ever have thought that stealing was a good idea? If only I could turn back time.

The shop assistant steps closer, bends to my eye level, and says, "I'm going to come to your home tonight, after work, and tell your parents everything. Then I'm going to your school to have your principal announce that you're a thief during the September first assembly."

My heart lurches, and my body starts to shake violently as the sobs overcome me and rip from my throat. I shield my face with my hands and moan. Mom is going to kill me!

"Apologize in front of our customers, then you can go," the shop assistant says coldly, tugging my hands off my face.

Everyone's watching me in stunned silence. There are at least a hundred people in the store now. How mortifying! If only I had an invisibility cloak.

The shop assistant nudges me forward. "Apologize."

"Sorry," I say, lowering my head.

"Look at everyone."

I raise my head back. "I'm sorry."

"Louder."

"I'm sorry," I yelp and run to the exit.

I hide behind a giant palm tree across the alley and collapse to the ground. I'm in so much trouble. Mom will wring my neck. I'll have to run away from home now.

Can I live in the forest? Since I got lost there last time, I'd say no. I was scared, not knowing whether I was walking toward the road or away from it. Every time the leaves moved, I thought it was a bear or a wolf or worse.

It would be much safer to swim across the sea to Turkey. If I get tired, I can just flip on my back and float for a while. Or . . . can I ask Dad for help? He's bailed me out of trouble so many times. He'll save the day again, I'm sure.

"Girl, you look troubled. Are you OK?" a lady passerby asks me. "You weren't even blinking."

"A terrible headache," I mutter hoarsely. I don't see her eyes through her blue sunglasses, but they must be kind.

"I know how bad a headache can feel," the woman says sympathetically. "Do you want me to walk you to your house?"

"No." I'm so down, I can't even muster a smile.

As the kind lady continues on her way, I drag my feet out from underneath me and get up. Time to find Dad.

I'm fortunate—he is in his room, pushing his big feet into his rubber boots. Near him stands a wooden basket.

"Going to collect mushrooms?" I ask, making Dad jump.

"Laura, you're back!" he exclaims. "Let's go to the mountain forest together."

"Fantastic," I say, trying to sound enthusiastic. "Let's go."

I'm going to the forest after all.

It takes our bus one hour to take us to the city's rural side. Dad grasps my hand and holds it firmly as we get off. The bus roars to life and puffs out a black cloud of funny-smelling gasses as a farewell.

Dad laughs long and loud. "Let's run."

Somehow nothing feels funny. I can't even pretend to laugh. When should I tell him?

"What were you thinking when you were looking out the window?" Dad asks.

"Just taking in the little houses with their flower gardens," I answer. "It must be nice to be able to plant your own flowers."

"If only I could buy a house and a garden for you."

He is walking so easily in his monstrously big boots. I have to half run to keep up and talk.

"The government has promised Mom a piece of land at the tea plantation for her service there," I say.

Dad doesn't reply, just continues marching us toward an opening in the trees. I suspect he's not replying because he doesn't really want me to live apart from him, and he knows *he* won't be invited.

"Did you have your own house when you were a kid?" I ask.

"Yes, my grandparents were well-off," Dad replies briskly.

"Oh, speaking of grandparents, a man on the bus thought you were my grandfather," I say, teasing him. "He said that you, my grandpa, raised me well when I offered him my seat."

"Moron," Dad mutters to himself.

"You're only fifty-seven," I say placatingly.

"Exactly."

The matter settled, I change the subject. "Will there be a lot of mushrooms today?"

"Plenty. After a rainy night like we had—definitely."

The long path beyond the opening gives way to the vast forest, and I scan the grass for the fat mushroom hats.

Dad points at small mushrooms lining a brook. "Watch out for those. They're poisonous."

"But beautiful," I note, staring at their lace-like stockings and red hats dotted with white spots.

"That's by design. To warn animals."

Dad grasps my hand more tightly, and we cross the bubbling brook, jumping on the rocks sticking up from the water, then go farther. Dad seems to know everything about everything in the forest.

When our basket is full of big, safe-to-eat mushrooms, we turn and go back the way we came. I have no idea how Dad always knows the right direction.

Oh God, I gotta do it.

"Have you ever stolen anything, Dad?" I ask quietly.

He thinks for a second before answering. "Yes, I have."

My heart flutters with relief. "What was it that you stole?"

He hesitates again before answering. "Pears from my neighbor's orchard."

I purse my lips. It's not what I hoped to hear. Every kid I know goes to the neighbors' gardens to get fruit. It can't compare to the real stealing I did. Dad won't understand me after all. Still, I have to confess.

"Dad, I stole a teddy bear today in Kids' World," I say with a sigh.

I wrap my arms around myself and wait for his reaction.

"Oh?" he asks, staring down at me.

I nod. "And the shop assistant caught me and made me apologize to the customers."

"She did *what*?"

"Made me—"

"What a b . . . bad person," he growls.

"But I . . . stole a toy, Dad."

"Laura, we should teach children through love, not humiliation."

I breathe out. "Won't you scold me at all?"

"Do you remember when you took a wallet from your mother's friend to play with her money?" he asks me.

"I was only three. Now I'm ten."

"But what did I do when I discovered that?"

"You took me to that friend's house, and we returned the money."

"Was that the right thing to do?" he asks softly.

"Yes," I reply.

"All of us make mistakes, Laura, and it's never too late to change ourselves for the better."

I decide not to tell Dad that I also stole a toy the day before, otherwise he'll go to the store and pay for it with the rest of his money. My dad is simply fantastic, so forgiving. I look up at him and smile.

He smiles back. "Do you want to hike to an ancient cave one of these days?"

"Yes to any offers and adventures," I reply eagerly.

"We also need to revisit the alpine meadows. Do you want to rest now? I have bread and water for a snack."

"I forgot I didn't eat all day."

"Let's find a stump and sit on it."

After we eat, we continue on our way. There's not much to do or talk about, so we walk in silence, maneuvering around the fallen trees, with Dad holding my hand. At some point, I spot a coiled snake in the grass, gigantic and long, silvery black. I jump in fright, whimpering, then place myself against Dad's shoulder.

"Shhh." Dad scoops me up under one arm and carries me a few steps backward, changing our direction.

I look suspiciously at the mossy trees around us. That's where snakes hide in movies.

"Now all the danger is behind you," Dad says, putting me down.

"If only . . ." I mutter grimly. Nothing about the shop assistant has really been resolved.

"What do you mean 'if only'?"

"The shop assistant said she'd come to our house tonight to talk to you and Mom."

"Then let her come . . . I'll be waiting," Dad says. Then he says no more.

Once home, we immediately start cooking. I peel potatoes happily and don't even get upset when I cut my hand with a knife.

Dad fries the mushrooms first to make the liquid evaporate, then adds thin potato slices. The aroma is knee-buckling. I close my eyes and breathe it in.

When the food is ready, Dad surprises me by inviting Mom to eat with us. I've never seen them spend time together. Sitting around the table as a family in our shabby kitchen is a first for us. Maybe we did it when Grandpa was alive; some vague memories stir in my mind.

I can't believe I'm witnessing Mom and Dad talking like an ordinary husband and wife, making an effort to be friendly to each other. I'm in awe. But how long will their truce last? And . . . am I just imagining things, or is Dad secretly in love with Mom?

After dinner, Mom volunteers to wash the dishes, and Dad and I go to his room. As I pass the front door, I surreptitiously glance at it. I was so preoccupied with the novelty of my parents talking to each other that I forgot to worry about the shop assistant. It seems too late for her to come now. Maybe she took pity on me or was too lazy to bother.

"You didn't notice the new TV in my room earlier, did you?" Dad asks.

"No," I reply. *I was preoccupied with other things.*

"Runia gave it to me this morning."

Oh, so Dad went to visit Runia today. The two friends are quite infamous in our city for their shenanigans. No one ever told me exactly what kind of shenanigans, but I heard that even the police officers were laughing their heads off during one of Dad and Runia's many run-ins with the law.

I plop on Dad's couch and watch as he turns the TV on, and it starts working. The picture is black and white. I can't believe I can now watch whatever I want, whenever I want. Actually, I've gotten used to living without a TV set, and I enjoy the quiet. It allows me to spend more time playing and in my imagination.

We start watching a brainless musical show, and soon Dad gets frustrated with the commercials. They come almost one after another, in five-minute intervals. When the scam company MMM asks the viewers to invest in the privatization vouchers the government has given to Russian citizens, Dad angrily throws his slipper at the TV.

Thankfully, we already sold our vouchers when I found a store that was buying them, so no one will swindle us.

Calling it a night and waving goodnight to Dad, I go into Mom's and my room and flop on my bed, waiting for sleep to come. It doesn't. I pull my blanket up to my neck and count the fluffy sheep in my mind. It doesn't work. I'm too wired after the day I had. Maybe counting the letters in the name Barbie will help. Now that my plans to earn money for her have been dashed, thinking of it is all I have.

The first letter in the word Barbie is *b*, and it's the second letter of the alphabet. *A* is the first, *r* eighteenth, *b* second again, *I* ninth, and *e* is the fifth. Adding up the numbers of the letters' places in the alphabet, I get thirty-seven. Three plus seven equals ten. One plus zero—one. So Barbie's number, according to my numerology, is one.

Ugh, I'm still not sleepy. *Barbie doll.* I want it so much. How frustrating that I can't have it and that I can't hold it.

I get out of bed, grab a pen and a sheet of paper, and go to the kitchen, where I turn the light on, sit at the table, and begin to write.

Dear God,

It's me, Laura. Thank you for the sun, moon, and trees. Thank you for my parents and for me. You are very powerful and can do anything.

I don't usually ask you for stuff, because I know you have more important things to do. But I'd like to ask you now because I want a Barbie doll so much. Could you please send me one? Pretty please?

I love you,
Your Laura

Putting my pen down, I stand up, spray a few water droplets from the sink on the top of my paper, and walk over to the window. I climb on the sill and stick the letter to the upper part of the glass pane so God can read it.

I feel a gentle nudge on my foot. I glance down and see Doll. My sweetheart of a dog is looking at me with her big, soulful brown eyes, wagging her tail.

I slide back to the floor and bend down to kiss her. "Hey, my pumpkin."

I pick her up and spin her around. There's no better doll in the world than my Doll. She's a teddy bear and a doll, all in one. What else could I want?

A Dream Come True

"Laura, wake up." I hear Mom's musical voice but don't want to fully wake up. I press my face into the pillow and try to fall back asleep.

"Sleepyhead, wake up." Mom nudges me on the shoulder. "I have a surprise for you."

I slowly open my eyes. I like surprises. What is it? As my vision clears, I find myself face-to-face with a blue-eyed, curly-haired Barbie doll. *Barbie.*

I jump out of bed and hug Mom. "Thank you, thank you, thank you."

"You're welcome," Mom responds, flustered by my sudden outburst.

I touch the translucent pink box in her hands and study Barbie's gown. It's long, white like a wedding dress, and covered with teeny-tiny rhinestones.

"But how did you get Barbie?" I whisper.

"After I saw your letter in the window, I went to the bank and withdrew my savings."

I squeeze her waist tightly in gratitude, then take the Barbie box out of her hands and step back. I sink to the floor, untying the ribbon around the box and opening the lid, then carefully pulling out the doll. Tall and slender, she's simply gorgeous. I touch her silky hair reverently and run my finger over her face. She's real.

Still holding my Barbie in amazement, I throw on some clothes and head out for a walk around the city. I'm going to show my Barbie to the whole world. I lift it up at shoulder level and walk out the door.

As I stroll along the streets, I do slow turnarounds every hundred yards, making sure that everyone can see my doll. When I pass the Central Market, I look at the Georgian sweets, churchkhelas, hanging in colorful rows like Christmas garlands and realize how hungry I am. I remember their taste. They're made of sweet, thickened grape juice that's chewy even with the added hazelnuts and walnuts.

I stop at a drinking fountain at the side of the market square and catch water with my mouth. The more I drink, the less hunger I'll feel. I've been using this trick for a long time.

From the corner of my eye, I spot a bus coming in my direction. I trot to the bus stop, and as the bus approaches and its doors fold open, I hop onto it.

I settle in a seat at the back window and, once en route, start watching the busy business district of the city roll by. At the final stop, the driver leaves for a cigarette break, but I decide to stay and go for another round. It'll be fun to watch the different streets through the window while the bus passengers are gawking at my Barbie.

But when the driver returns, he notices me through the rear-view mirror.

"Do you have a ticket?" he inquires, adjusting the mirror to see me better. His pinkie fingers have very long nails. I don't know why.

"Do you have a ticket?" he repeats.

I make a nonchalant face, pretending to be deaf and dumb. Kids ride buses for free all the time. What's wrong with him? Is he a Scrooge McDuck?

The other passengers start piling in, and I decide to slip off the bus after all.

I'm glad I did. It's a really pretty day, and lots of people are out walking with their dogs. Some families are enjoying this warm day with picnics spread on the lush grass of the city garden. I can really show my Barbie off to them.

Now I also hear children's music playing loudly somewhere in the distance. A concert maybe? I listen closer for the exact direction, then start walking toward it. It's somewhere in the seaport.

"Hey!" someone shouts behind me as I step onto the sidewalk.

I turn and see a group of three girls about my age. I smile at them. "My name's Laura. Let's play together."

"You have no taste," one of the girls grumbles, furrowing her narrow forehead, looking me up and down.

"Your T-shirt is the color of poop," a girl who resembles the first says.

"And the blue shorts . . ." adds the third girl. She looks different than the other two girls, more muscular. Is she a sporty girl?

All three girls stop and glare at my Barbie. Yes, at least she's dressed perfectly. I look down at myself. They're right; my clothes don't match, but I've never thought about choosing them by color. Why bother?

I look back at the girls and scan their clothes. The first girl is wearing a tight white dress and navy suede shoes, the second girl some shapeless purple garment and silver shoes, and the third a green dress and almost invisible flesh-colored shoes. All the colors of their clothes go well with each other.

Disappointed that they're not interested in playing with me, I turn away and hurry on my way to the crosswalk.

"Give us that Barbie!" they shout, and I hear running steps behind me.

Panicked, I look around for someone to protect me. There's a woman on a nearby sidewalk. I veer off in her direction.

"Ma'am, help!" I yell. "The girls want to take my doll."

"Oh no, you don't," the woman shouts at them, her pink hat flopping from her indignation. "Leave this girl alone!"

The three girls sprint across the road to the other side like the cowards that they are and disappear around a small building nearby.

My lady savior walks for a few seconds ahead of me, then gives me a cheerful smile and continues on her way in the other direction. I take my time by detouring through a palm garden, making sure the girls don't come back. After counting five minutes in my head, I set off toward the seaport.

Close to an enormous cruise ship docked at its pier, a small stage has been erected temporarily, and hundreds of kids are performing—dancing and singing—while their parents and teachers cater to them. And there are those three girls standing behind the stage, changing out of their clothes and pulling on yellow chick costumes while an adult nearby counts the heads of all the children present there. So, the three girls are dancers . . . They were certainly right to give me fashion advice. *Great outfits, ladies.*

I don't want these yellow chickens to run after me and my Barbie when they see me, so I leave, sprinting to the underpass and reappearing on the other side of Voykova Street.

In my courtyard, three boys I know are playing ball. They're dressed in shorts that look more like cotton briefs, but I decide not to tease them about it. I'm not like those mean girls.

The boys ignore me and continue kicking their ball against a neighbor's wall, then jumping over it fast as it ricochets back. That poor neighbor, the noise must be headache-inducing.

I know why these boys are ignoring me. I actually started that. In the past, Stephen, Simon, Max, and I were inseparable as friends, but after they started calling me a boy for hanging out with them, I began avoiding them.

I stick my Barbie out in front of me and slowly walk past them. *I'm not a boy.*

Back at the apartment, I place my Barbie on the table near my bed and go to Dad's room. He's on our balcony.

"Are you building something?" I ask, looking at the orange bricks he's arranged in piles of four.

"I'm helping to finish the summer cottage for Mrs. Orlova," he replies.

Alaina Orlova is our neighbor and a famous host of multiple TV shows. I was at her apartment once and saw big boxes of candies on the tables. She's rich.

"She gave you a beef patty sandwich," Dad tells me. "It's in the kitchen."

"Awesome," I say and dart back across Dad's room.

Sitting at the kitchen table, I bite into the sandwich. I'm blown away by how delicious it is, even cold. I try to listen to my inner voice and leave half of the beef patty for the dogs, but I can't help my hunger and take another bite and another. *Stop!*

"I'll leave a piece of patty in the dogs' bowls," I yell.

"The rats will come and eat it," Dad yells back. "Put it in my fridge."

Oh, yes, rats . . . they've already stolen my dogs' squeaky toy. I heard its telltale sounds coming from the basement. They were playing with it. The nerve of them!

After I drink some water, I return to the courtyard. Mrs. Yermol is there, and she tells me that Sveta, a tourist from Arkhangelsk, is in the front yard of the power station that adjoins our apartment building.

I run there and find her doing gymnastics on the concrete floor, which is raised up, just like a small stage.

"Hi," I say and sit on the edge of the floor to watch her.

Now she's walking upside down on her hands and feet like a crab, her long, tanned legs stretched. She flips them over her head and straightens up. Sveta has grown up since the last time I saw her. I think she turned twelve this year.

I swallow my envy at her flexibility and ask, "Practicing?"

"Yes, for my Olympic reserve school," she replies.

"Isn't your skirt too short for practice?"

"It'll do." She smiles, and her stretched lips instantly remind me of a tilted crescent moon.

"Show me more things you can do."

Continuing to smile, she rotates her clutched hands from her back over her head and to the front. How is this possible?

I'm about to try to repeat this trick when a boy from the small apartment building next to ours appears on the stairs to our stage.

"Girls!" he exclaims, as if he's never seen girls before.

It looks like he's wearing his dad's pants, two sizes too large, so they're tied with a long shoelace. We wave at him silently.

"What are you doing?" he asks.

"Is your name Ivan?" I ask him.

"Yes, it's Ivan."

"We're doing gymnastics," I say, including myself in the cool thing.

"You'll never believe what I just did," he says. "I stole a few bricks from the truck parked over there."

I look in the direction he's pointing and hear the engine roaring loudly to life. The truck is leaving. My brain suddenly makes a connection between the bricks and my dad.

Collecting myself, I ask, "If I tell you the bricks are my dad's, will you return them?"

"Shoot," Ivan says. "Are they?"

"Yes."

"Stop the truck, and I'll retrieve the bricks from the bushes."

Sveta starts running ahead of me, moving up the driveway and to the road above, and I follow her.

"Dad," I shout. "Wait!"

Thankfully, he or the driver hears me, and the truck stops. Dad jumps out of the passenger's side. "What's up?"

I don't have to reply. Ivan is walking toward us, carrying the bricks, struggling to keep his back straight. Sveta and I run to help him.

"He borrowed them for a few minutes to play," I explain to Dad.

"Stole them, more like," Ivan says.

"Thank you for your honesty," Dad says immediately, clapping him on the shoulder approvingly.

Ivan beams at him.

Dad fishes a few bills out of his coverall's pocket and hands it to me. "Three ice cream cones for all of you."

Ivan and I turn and run to the store, not waiting for Sveta, who takes her time balancing on her hands. For once she stops showing off and runs like a cheetah to catch up with us.

"Your dad is an angel," Ivan says to me. "My dad would have whipped my butt with a belt."

"I'm more afraid of my mother," I say honestly. "Although she only beat me once."

"What did you do?" Sveta asks me.

"I sang a song about being in love with a much older man. She thought I invented the lyrics, but I heard them on the radio."

She chuckles and then says, "I've never been punished."

"My dad says physical punishment builds character in kids," Ivan says.

"No, it's wrong," Sveta responds.

"So, Ivan, what did you want to do with those bricks?" I ask.

"Build a fire pit for roasting potatoes," he answers.

"Oh wow, that would have been yummy," Sveta says. "Can you use big rocks from the beach instead?"

"I'll think about it."

In the store, I buy a Bounty chocolate bar instead of ice cream and wait for the others to make their purchases.

"Today is my lucky day," I declare on our way back.

"How so?" asks Sveta.

"Mom bought me a Barbie doll today."

"Let's play with it. I'll bring mine."

"Great idea."

Ivan's expression goes sour, and he shakes his head. "I'm out."

He picks up his pace and disappears from sight behind a cluster of houses at the side of the road.

We laugh and go to my apartment to get my Barbie, then go to her apartment, and afterward, we knock on the other girls' doors, telling them to come out into the courtyard with their dolls.

All in all, there are seven of us by the evening—seven of us and seven of our Barbies. Two sisters, Olivia and Polina, who themselves look like brown-haired dolls, bring a quilt for us to sit on and tiny toy outfits.

As night draws closer, the girls' parents start calling for them to go home, one by one, and we reluctantly part. I'm the only one left in the courtyard, looking at my friends' windows, seeing the inviting glow of their lamps. My parents never call for me. I'm free to come home whenever I want and to hang outside as much as I want. Everyone envies me for that, but secretly, I want to be called home on time too.

Chapter Eight
Monsters

The following day, I wake up exhausted. I've been sewing clothes for my Barbie half the night. She's still on my table and hasn't disappeared.

Smiling, I go to the kitchen and make myself a sugar sandwich. Still feeling hungry afterward, I decide to fry potatoes.

"Want me to do that?" Dad asks, coming into the kitchen. He looks energetic and radiant today. I like to see him like this, sober.

"Yes, please," I agree eagerly.

"Do you want me to add eggs to your potatoes?" he offers.

I shrug. "I'll give it a try. When is it going to be ready?"

"In thirty minutes or so."

"I'll go for a walk while I wait."

On my way to the courtyard, I envision the living things inhabiting the gardens I'm passing by: voles, beetles, grasshoppers, ladybugs, moths, birds . . .

As I round the corner, I see a little boy, not more than six years old, playing with his enormous, floppy-eared dog. It must be super hot for the dog in the summer, with so much fur. But oh my, it must be the most beautiful and massive dog I've ever seen.

"What breed is it?" I ask, approaching the boy.

"Saint Bernard," the boy answers, squaring his small shoulders proudly.

"Lucky you. What a colorful teddy bear to cuddle with!"

"True. Do you want a dog like this?"

"I already have two dogs."

"What breed are they?"

"Royal pooch," I joke.

"Royal what?" he asks.

"Mongrels. They're mongrels."

From the corner of my eye, I see a figure running down our driveway. The figure's light brown hair is flapping like a parachute behind it. I turn and recognize my good friend Victoria behind the wild locks. Woo-hoo!

I run toward her, give her a big high five, then lead her across the courtyard to the bench. Traitorously, my gaze slips to the can of Coca-Cola in her hand.

"How can you drink that dangerous stuff?" I ask, scrunching my nose, pretending to be disgusted.

Victoria looks at the can thoughtfully, then unexpectedly pours the unfinished drink into the bush behind the bench. My jaw drops, and the Scrooge in me rears its greedy head. I secretly wanted that Coca-Cola.

Victoria places the empty can under the bench, then looks at the top part of the driveway and gestures for me to look there too. A tall, thin woman is half walking, half dancing toward our courtyard. *Who's that?*

As she goes through our courtyard, her behavior becomes even more bizarre. Dancing on her tiptoes, she starts doing elaborate movements with her arms. Despite our loud gasps, she pays no attention to us, just continues on her way to the street stairs.

"Her eyes are glassy, like a zombie's," Victoria notices.

"Have you seen her before?" I ask.

"No, but I heard about her. She dreamed of becoming a ballerina, but her dream was crushed, and she went mad."

"Mad," I repeat in utter horror.

"Yes, she lost her marbles. She thinks she's performing. Once when kids were throwing tomatoes at her, she bowed to them, thinking the tomatoes were flowers."

"That's sad." I sigh, lowering my head. *Is my mother also like that?* No, not like *that*, for sure.

"Let's go visit Anastasia," Victoria says, trying to cheer us back up. "She's just returned from Saint Petersburg."

We get up and go to Anastasia's courtyard near baby Sophia's house. A bunch of teen girls are playing ball there, dressed in neon pink leggings and denim skirts. I definitely want a pair of Lycra leggings like that. Any color will do.

Victoria takes my hand and tugs me to the wooden building on the farther corner of the driveway. I hope Anastasia has forgotten the day she got poisoned because of me. It happened when I found a chocolate bar in a pile of debris at a construction site. I shared only one piece with her and ate the rest myself. Later that afternoon, Anastasia was taken to the hospital. The chocolate probably had been saturated with dangerous chemicals from the building site.

I was OK till evening, then hammers started banging inside my skull, making me violently ill.

Dad reacted like the goofy dad he is, by going to Mrs. Yermol and asking her to bake apple pastries for me. I couldn't even look at them, let alone eat them.

"Where are you going?" Victoria asks me.

So deep in thought, I've passed Anastasia's house entirely. I return and wait for Victoria to pull the heavy door of the entrance open, then both of us walk into a decrepit stairwell. Some stairs go up and some down. As we start climbing them to the second floor, we hear a sudden, loud crash coming from the basement. We freeze.

"It must be the old ghost," Victoria whispers, sounding scared. "Anastasia told me about it."

Terrified, I turn and run back downstairs. One step, two, three . . . the glossy surface is slippery, and I desperately try not to lose my balance. But nothing helps. My arms flail, and I fall, hitting the stairs with my face.

My eyes water in pain. I immediately touch my mouth—half of my front tooth is missing. Darn it, I've cracked it off.

Victoria rushes over to me—the ghost is forgotten—and starts dragging me up to my feet. "Poor Laura. Let's get out of here."

I keep touching my broken tooth as we walk back to my courtyard. It hurts in a weird way, but nothing else hurts. There's no blood or anything. The whole ordeal must have been just to punish me or to teach me a lesson. Something like: *Believe in God; don't believe in ghosts.*

Victoria looks at my tooth apologetically. "Did you pick the broken part from the floor?"

"No," I reply. "Why would I?"

"Maybe a dentist can glue it together?"

"Pff, no."

"But you won't be able to smile."

"Don't care," I say. "What should we do now?"

"Wanna make clover crowns?" Victoria offers.

I nod and follow her to the lawn near Dad's garden. I notice that a lot of plants are growing tall there now after we sowed seeds in the spring. What is it about the end of August that makes them sprout and grow so fast?

Avoiding bees, Victoria and I search for clover blooms in the grass. Just the thought of a bee sting is enough to hurt.

I sit on an oak tree's roots and wave for Victoria to sit next to me. She drops a bunch of flowers in my lap and squats in front of me, then starts braiding the tiny flowers into bunches of three.

"That's how you do it," she says.

It's so exciting—I'm able to repeat after her. And it's amazing how many things can be made by hand from anything and everything.

"I like Ava's brother," Victoria says, breaking the silence.

"George?" I ask.

"Who else?"

"I like him too."

"No, you don't get it. I really like him."

I clap a hand over my mouth. "But he's in love with Mia."

"Pity," she says.

"I'd like to have him as my brother," I say, "so he'd protect me."

Victoria smiles and rises to her feet. "I need to go home and use the bathroom."

"Just do it here, in the bushes," I suggest.

"Nope. I need toilet paper."

"What a ninny!"

She cracks up laughing but still leaves. I put my crown on my head and go to the street stairs, then step down to a huge white mulberry tree by the roadside.

When I pull a branch toward me to pick the berries, I suddenly remember the potatoes and eggs Dad is cooking for me. I let the branch go, leap back onto the stairs, and sprint home.

Dad is in his room, watching TV, and a pan of fried potatoes sits on the small table in front of him. I slump next to him on the couch and start to eat.

The whole egg concoction smells like the sulfur on match heads. It's quite tasty, but with each forkful, the eggs seem to stand in the way of the utter deliciousness of the fries.

After I finish eating them, Dad brings me fresh flatbread and a glass of milk. These two tastes blend perfectly. The bread almost melts in my mouth as I chew and sip milk simultaneously. I could swear milk makes bread sweet. Mmm, yummy.

"You have a beautiful crown," Dad notes.

I touch the clover flowers on my head and smile wide. "Yeah."

"What happened to your tooth?" Dad asks with alarm.

"I fell and chipped it. It'll grow back." *I hope.*

Dad wrinkles his forehead, looking unconvinced. "Is the tooth sensitive to the food now?"

I pause to think. "No, not at all."

Dad sighs and shifts his eyes back to the TV.

I wipe the crumbs off my face and stand up. "I'm going back outside."

"Be careful," he grumbles.

"OK."

As I sprint toward the courtyard, a wave of sudden sadness sweeps over me. Intuition maybe, or I probably feel unwell because I've overeaten.

The older ladies have finally come out into the courtyard and now are sitting on the bench, nibbling on their freshly fried sunflower seeds. At first, I go toward them, then change my direction, deciding to just walk around the neighborhood, playing by myself.

I listlessly walk up toward the road above, talking to myself, imagining myself being an adult and having a daughter who's walking by my side.

"Mom," I say in a little-girl voice. "Buy me an ice cream cone, please."

"Sorry, sweetie," I reply in a grown-woman voice. "I don't have money."

I open my imaginary wallet and show my imaginary daughter the nonexistent contents. "See? My wallet is empty."

Before I can continue my dialogue, I feel a gaze on me. Turning, I see a man sitting in a Zhiguli car, gaping at me. His long, red beard seems even longer with his mouth hanging open. He's shocked. No doubt he thinks I'm a lunatic, moving my arms in the air, talking to someone who isn't there. I zip past him, jumping into the bushes of someone's garden.

On the other side of the garden, there's a small grove. I continue walking and wind up in someone's courtyard. I hope they don't mind me hanging out here. I saunter in circles, examining the chalk drawings on the pavement. Some pieces of chalk are still scattered around.

Making sure the coast is clear, I pick up a piece of purple chalk and start drawing a girl's face. It almost looks real.

Someone gasps beside me, and I snap my head up.

"Oh, I thought you were an old lady who didn't feel well," the woman says, holding her hand over her heart. Her other hand is holding a wooden xylophone. I've only seen one in pictures before.

"I'm taking it to my grandson's day care," she says, noticing my gaze. "They're preparing a show."

She gives me a small talk on being aware of my surroundings, and I hang on her every word because I think this is useful stuff. When we part ways, I go to the lawn nearby to pick a few gooseberries from the bushes. Afterward, I meander through the streets, heading for the bus stop near the flagpoles. One of the buses will eventually bring my mother from work, so I'll meet her there.

A few people mill around at the bus stop, waiting. I stand with them, watching their grim, unsmiling expressions and their distant, unseeing stares, then I go to the public garden nearby to play. After getting bored again, I hop into one gray telephone booth and dial a random phone number.

The person who answers is a good sport and plays along as I talk to them. I pretend to be their daughter and ask them for strawberries, laughing and laughing.

Remembering a phone prank my friends told me about, I decide to try it, so I dial another random phone number.

"Hello," I say when a woman takes my call. "Do you need a TV set?"

"No," she replies.

"OK, then we'll come to your house and take it out."

I hang up and immediately realize that the joke was mean. *Enough.*

I almost miss Mom's silhouette among the others when she arrives. I run after her and hug her from behind. "Gotcha!"

She squeals. "I never know where you're going to pop up."

She opens her bag, showing me a plastic plate with cabbage and sausage stew. "Look what I have."

"The lunch they gave you at work?" I ask.

"Yes. This one was easy to bring to you."

Mom is lucky—her employer, the state farm, feeds their workers for free, and sometimes, like today, Mom is able to bring food home.

As we walk toward the apartment building, I suddenly remember about my tooth. Opening my mouth like a growling dog, I say, "I fell and broke my tooth today."

Mom gasps. "It's your permanent tooth. But don't worry, when the rest of your baby teeth fall out, we'll go to a dentist."

"So it won't grow back?"

"No."

Laura with a crooked tooth it is then.

Even more food awaits us at home. Mrs. Zayka brought us pea soup and left it in our kitchen. Our darling neighbor keeps bringing us soup even after Mom yelled at her for it. It all happened one time after Dad poured out Mom's meat soup, saying that Mrs. Zayka's Ukrainian borscht tasted much better.

How could it have been Mrs. Zayka's fault? I'd wanted to cry with pity for her as she had to endure a barrage of my mother's insults. What a cruel punishment for her kindness.

If not for Mrs. Zayka, we wouldn't even have had food for the past New Year's celebration. Besides, borscht is the most delicious soup, hands down.

I try to forget the painful, disappointing memory and go to the kitchen to turn on the stove. I'll eat Mom's food today because I know how much trouble she went to bringing it to me.

I lick the tomato paste off my lips after finishing everything on the plate and scurry to the bedroom. Clambering into the bed beside Mom, I listen to her read passages from an English textbook. The language sounds enchanting.

Mom starts to caress my hair, and I press myself into her warm shoulders.

"Sleep, my joy, sleep," she croons.

Yes, I'm going to sleep next to her tonight. Closing my eyes, I let my mind drift.

Something wakes me up in the middle of the night. I sit upright and listen. All I hear is the pounding of my heart. Then it comes—*thump, thump, thump.*

It sounds like Dad is banging his large axe on our door. He's trying to break it down. Even the windowpanes are vibrating.

Thump, thump, thump.

"I'm going to kill you, Talia!" Dad bellows from the other side of the door, slurring his words.

A current runs through me. I tug the blanket up to my neck. Dad scares me. The darkness in the room scares me too. *Why, God? I was sleeping. Why can't I just sleep?*

My eyes adjust to the darkness, and I look up at Mom, who's sitting next to me. She's staring at the door as if the sheer force of her stare can keep the door from cracking.

Thump, thump, thump.

"I'll kill you!" Dad yells again.

He's obviously drunk; that's when he gets aggressive and violent toward Mom.

The door is now jerking from Dad's force. I don't think it'll break, though. Mom just recently installed it to protect us from Dad. It only looks wooden—its core is metal. Also, Mom installed safety bars on our window so that we can unlock them and escape the room if we need to.

Thump, thump, thump.

"Daddy, please stop!" I beg in a gentle voice, then squeeze my eyes shut and wait for the next blow to come.

Thump. Thump.

"Dad, please!" I plead again.

Thump.

"Daaad, pleeease!" I cry out.

Silence, except for the sound of the crickets outside. The floorboards creak, and Dad's door closes. *He's gone.*

I feel queasy. Mom kisses my forehead gently and lets out a warm sigh of relief, then we both lie down on her pillow.

For a long time, I can't fall asleep. I just lie there, tossing and turning softly. The air has a peculiar sound to it. Why haven't I noticed it before? Everything around us is buzzing. I concentrate on it and concentrate, and the next thing I know, it's morning.

Chapter Nine
Saviors

Our room is filled with the sun's rays. I try to catch the thick strips. What a warm feeling the sunlight gives my palms, almost like a tickle or a massage.

Reluctantly, I climb out from under Mom's warm green blanket and head for the bathroom. I pause in the corridor and turn to look at our door. Deep cuts from the axe are strewn all over the varnished surface. I step closer and touch the marks with my hand. They're big and wide.

I turn away and pause to look at my reflection in the mirror—disheveled sandy hair chopped in uneven layers, slanting eyes, green irises, and Mom's full lips that my classmates call dumplings. I don't look like Barbie at all.

Disappointed, I run to the kitchen, grab a pair of scissors, and trim the uneven layers of hair around my face. There, I feel better now. I return to the corridor, flip on the bathroom lights, and walk in.

I'd better take a bath soon, or our neighbors will again complain to my mom that my skin is smudged with dirt. As I reach to twist the faucet, I feel something brush against my ankle. I look down and scream. There's a fat gray rat running around in panic, trying to find a hole to dash into but instead colliding with the corners of the room.

I jump into the bathtub and scream again. Come to think of it, that was a mistake. Now I'm trapped with the rat in this small, six-foot-long room.

The bathroom door flies open, and Dad charges in. Seeing the rat, he steps toward it and taps the floor with his gigantic rubber boot. The rat turns and launches toward the exit, but instead of escaping through the wide-open door, it jumps right into Dad's boot.

He starts howling like I've never seen him do before. He hops back into the corridor, stamping his foot and stamping, almost dancing. I climb out of the bathtub and watch Dad in horror. I hope the rat won't bite him.

Finally, the rodent leaps out of the boot, and as Dad kicks at it, the rat jumps five feet high, then runs through Dad's room, onto the glass balcony, and out the open window.

How is it possible for a rat to jump so high? And I thought I was safe from it in the bathtub.

"It didn't bite you, did it?" I ask Dad.

"Noooo," he whines, and we both burst out laughing.

"I once saw a rat's teeth when it jumped out of a dumpster and bared them at me, so you're lucky this rat didn't bite you."

We're both silent now. Should I broach the subject and ask him about yesterday? He never talks about things like that. Does he even remember it? I wish he'd quit drinking. It seems so easy. *Or is it?*

After breakfast, I slip into my white and blue sundress and head for the courtyard. As I expected, no one's here this early, so I gallop up the driveway and down the street to the small white house where my friend Peter lives. I haven't seen him all summer. Why did he stop coming?

"Who are you?" asks an older woman guarding the entrance.

"Peter's friend," I answer.

"That snotnose!" she says, cackling hoarsely, revealing her expensive golden teeth.

Snotnose? Peter? I only associate his nose with how crooked it is ever since he broke it in a fight. I guess this woman has known Peter since he was a toddler.

I continue on my way toward the stairs and can't help but imagine green snot stuck to Peter's nose like goo. It's not an image I wanna have in my head.

I stop in front of door number eight and knock quietly. It opens almost immediately, and Peter's un-snotty nose appears in the crack.

He sighs when he sees me. "My parents forbade me to be friends with you."

That stings. "Why?"

"Quiet," he hisses. "My parents are home."

"Did you tell them about the time I put you in the dumpster?" I whisper, feeling betrayed. "I was just kidding."

"No, I didn't," he whispers back.

I narrow my eyes at him. "When you hit my head with your toy gun, I didn't tell on you. Wait . . . did you tell them about the time we got locked out on the roof of my apartment building?"

Peter shakes his head. "No. It was the police who told my parents that you talked me into running away from home."

"But we had so much fun before they caught us."

Peter looks at me like I'm an idiot.

I jut out my chin. "So you won't be my friend anymore?"

"The heck I won't!" he says. "Wait for me in your courtyard."

He closes the door in my face, and I stay on the landing, shocked. That's not what I was expecting him to say, for sure.

Ungluing my feet, I run to my courtyard and sit down on the bench. Soon, Peter appears in the driveway, and I hop off the bench to hide in the passageway. As he comes closer, I jump in front of him and growl. He doesn't even bat an eyelid, not scared at all. That's not how I'd have reacted.

"Let's play hide-and-seek," he suggests.

"Let's," I say. "Who's going to be *It*?"

"You."

I smirk. "I promise your turn will come soon enough."

Biting the inside of my cheek in an effort not to smile, I go to the farthest corner of the courtyard, cover my eyes with my palms, and start counting. "One, two, three, four . . ."

When I reach one hundred—plenty of time to hide on another planet—I start walking across the courtyard, scanning it. Certainly, Peter isn't dumb enough to hide here. My intuition prompts me to go down the street stairs to the courthouse's gardens, the best place to hide, with many trees and plenty of greenery.

First, I check around the fountain there, the same fountain where I once hid from the angry rooster who'd attacked me. It also holds good memories for me. Dad once built a mini boat for me, and I sailed here, paddling with my arms.

Peter is nowhere to be seen, however. I change direction and walk through a grove toward my favorite camellia garden, where hundreds of green bushes grow, blooming with beautiful crimson flowers under the shadowy canopy of tall trees around. The whole place looks like a scene from a fairy tale.

As I continue walking, I notice a man sitting under a eucalyptus tree, with a cane propped next to him. I forgot how many a creep can hide here. I start walking backward.

The man has the audacity to wiggle his finger, summoning me. I flash my middle finger at him.

"My kitten got lost in the grass here," he says, getting up to his feet. "Please help me find it."

I pause and tilt my head, suddenly feeling ashamed of my rudeness. "You lost your kitten here?"

"Yes."

The man is dressed well, in a clean white linen suit. Of course he can't be a creep. I'll help him find his pet.

"Sir, you forgot your cane," I say to him as he starts limping toward me.

He shakes his head. "I don't want to scare the kitten."

"What's its name?"

He hesitates for a moment before answering, "Jitty."

"What does it look like?"

"Umm . . . ginger."

I turn and start sweeping through the grass with my foot.

"Jitty, baby," I call. "Jitty, Jitty!"

Suddenly, the man grabs me from behind and lifts me off the ground.

"Aaaah!" I yell.

"Shhh, be quiet," he hisses, squeezing me with his rough hands.

Tightening his grip even more, he turns me around and presses me into the wall of the courthouse. His eyes are milky blue and spooky.

"Heeeelp!" I scream, thrashing and jerking with all my might. I can't believe he'd dare to do this next to the courthouse of justice, the main place where the law is practiced.

I manage to break free for a bare second, but then he drags me back and pins me in place. Unzipping his pants, he pulls out a big . . . *sausage*. Ugh! I wanna gag. I scream again.

"Quiet," he says, blasting me with his sour breath. "Be a good girl, and I won't hurt you."

I fill my lungs with air and prepare to yell again, but it stays in my throat. The man has just pulled a small silver knife from his rear pocket and now is pointing it at my stomach.

"Good girl," he coos in a sickeningly soft voice, his face red and sweaty now.

The man lifts the hem of my dress and traces his fingers up my thigh. *God, please help me!*

"Let her go!" a voice comes from the other side of the trees above. *Peter.*

I take this moment of distraction and yank my shoulder out from under the man's hand, then run up the hill and through the trees.

Peter is waiting for me on the road above, and as I reach him, the two of us run toward the street stairs and up. My legs feel like Jell-O, and I slide down to the ground when we finally reach the safety of the courtyard.

"That was some hide-and-seek," I murmur despondently.

"More like hide-and-sick," Peter quips.

I look at him, not believing he saved me. He's only eight years old. Peter's lips twitch at the corners under my gaze. He's proud of himself too.

"If that moron comes anywhere near me again," I say, "I'll boil water and pour it on him."

"My parents say that safety is in numbers," Peter notes. "Don't go into the court's gardens alone."

"But remember when we were little and played together, these creeps also came and tried to talk to us. So there's no safety in numbers."

"But they didn't touch us, did they?"

I shake my head, then shudder in disgust before asking, "What will we play now? Let's climb on the power station roof and watch everyone from there?"

"Nuh-uh," Peter replies.

"No perverts there. It's safe."

"Safe? The last time we were there, you pushed me off the roof."

"But I jumped after you, didn't I?"

Peter presses his hand to his forehead and laughs. "I hear my mom calling my name."

"No, she isn't," I say dryly. "Stay."

"See you tomorrow," he says and starts backing away. "I'll go play my dartboard game at home now."

I harrumph, then watch Peter disappear from view. After that, I go to my kitchen window and ask Dad for a glass of water.

"Are you playing with the girls in the backyard?" he asks, handing me a glass through the safety bars.

"What girls?" I ask, and then I hear the voices of my friends.

Hastily, I abandon my glass of water on the windowsill and race toward the sounds.

"Wait for me!" I yell.

"Laura," Olivia says excitedly as I round the corner.

"What are you playing?"

"Royals," Ava answers.

"You'll be our servant," Polina says.

"Yes," I agree immediately and move into position at the edge of the backyard.

I don't mind playing a servant. I'm the least pretty girl in my neighborhood. Only my mother was against me playing a servant. She said I was the most beautiful girl and should only play the queen. What a stupid fool she is to think I'm beautiful! It must be that spell where all mothers think their kids are the best.

I look at the girls around me and check who else is in. Our new tourist friends, the sisters Inness and Yana, are here. They're much taller than the rest of us, so they're going to play the male roles. Anastasia, the girl who lives in the scary "ghost" house, is using a soft bush as a throne today. No wonder she was chosen to play the queen—she's beautiful, almost as beautiful as her mother, who won a beauty pageant when she was a teenager. I think she won it thanks to her strong cheekbones. If I chew gum a lot, will my cheekbones grow like that?

"Are we ready to play?" Ava asks us.

"Yes," we all say and start improvising.

About an hour into the game, we pause to gather and throw away the wolfberries growing in the grass. We believe they are poisonous, although Inness assures us that they're not. But just in case, we finish our task. Keeping the animals safe is important.

"Have you seen Peter's mom recently?" Olivia asks us. "She looks like she swallowed a watermelon."

"You mean she's pregnant?" Inness asks her.

"I wonder if Peter knows," I say. "I was just hanging out with him, and he didn't mention it."

"Boys . . ." Yana says in her almost-adult voice.

A loud whirring noise starts above our heads, and we look up. A huge helicopter is flying so low that I can see its shining propeller.

The neighbors open their windows to watch it too. The helicopter lifts all the dust from the ground as it flies by, hitting us with a big swooshing whirl.

It takes a few minutes for everyone to clear their eyes. Some neighbors' laundry hanging on the clothesline is ruined now.

"What was that?" Ava asks.

"Maybe they're looking for criminals?" I suggest, thinking of the pervert back in the courthouse's grove. I hope they're looking for him.

"I need to wash my eyes," Anastasia says. "I'm going home."

"We're too," Polina says, taking Olivia's hand.

"Just try to cry, and it'll help," I suggest.

"No, it won't work," Inness says in her smart-person tone.

I tag along with everyone to the building's stairs and decide to go home too. In my entrance hall, I stop. A woman is leaning against my front door, pressing her ear to it. A robber? The one who climbed through the window and stole Mom's crystal vase last month?

The woman senses my gaze and turns. I laugh to myself. It's just Mrs. Zayka, not a robber. I start walking again.

"Is it Talia singing?" Mrs. Zayka asks breathlessly.

I frown, confused. *What is she talking about?* Then I hear the singing—Mom's singing.

"She has such a lovely voice," Mrs. Zayka gushes.

"Yes, it's my mom," I say, feeling my cheeks become hot. "She likes to sing Tina Turner and Alla Pugacheva songs."

"Her voice sounds like a deep soprano."

Deep what? I suddenly remember that it took me a while to realize singers can also speak. I was sure singers were a special species of humans and could only sing.

"I wonder why Talia didn't try to become a singer," Mrs. Zayka murmurs.

Where would Mom start? At the concert hall doors? Knocking on them and telling the person who opens them she can sing? I doubt that.

I sidestep Mrs. Zayka and open my front door. Waving goodbye, I close it and follow Mom's voice into the bathroom.

She's standing bent over a plastic tub, doing laundry, looking young and happy, singing.

"Mrs. Zayka said you have a lovely voice," I tell her.

Mom jumps in surprise. "You sneaked up on me again."

"Uh-huh."

Collecting herself, Mom asks, "Really?"

"Mm-hmm."

"Did she actually, actually say that?" Pleasure is written all over her face.

"Yes," I reply in a firm voice, then relate every detail.

"No wonder. I have six hundred professions, and singer is one of them."

Wh-what? Mom's imagination has started running wild again, but I decide to humor her.

"What other professions do you have?" I ask.

"Breakdance teacher," she answers in a deadpan voice, her imagination not quitting.

How can I not laugh right now? Just picturing my mother twirling on the floor, performing breakdance moves, makes me want to shake with giggles. *Oh, Mom!* Though . . . I can use this story to awe my friends. If they don't believe me, I'll tell them to go and ask my mother.

I relax my on-the-verge-of-laughter expression and change the subject. "Is Dad at home?"

"No." Mom makes a sour face. "I was waiting for you, actually, so we could go to the police station to report him."

Why bother reporting him? The police only give Dad warnings, nothing else. Time after time. Nothing changes. Besides, I don't want Dad in jail. Although . . . it would probably be good for him—he wouldn't be able to drink.

Dad's bad habit has been getting more out of hand lately. Last month, I saw him kneeling in front of a neighbor, barefoot, begging to lend money to buy vodka. Dad's heels were dirty, and he looked so pathetic. Yes, prison would be good for him.

The decision made, I tug at my mother's arm. "Let's go."

It's almost the end of the workday when we arrive at the police station. The sprawling building is bustling with activity. I stay outside and wait for Mom as she goes through the main entrance.

The Arts and Culture Theater is on the other side of the road. I stare wistfully at its sculptural white walls, daydreaming about dancing there. I'd like to do something that's related to music, even if it's just playing piano.

I look at the police station again. Not more than five minutes have passed, but I'm bored and curious, so I go to the partially open door and peek inside.

Mom is talking to a police officer sitting in a protective glass cubicle behind his big wooden desk. Mom's telling him about all the times Dad has tried to kill her, but the officer stares at her with indifference.

"I'm sorry, ma'am," he says, furrowing his wide forehead, which has a big scar in the shape of the letter *c*. "We can't arrest your husband without some proof."

"As always, you ignore my plea for help," Mom says, sounding unusually calm. *Oh no, they're not going to help her.* I start twisting my arms nervously.

"Last time you told me that what goes on between a husband and wife is their own business," Mom goes on, "that—"

"Ma'am," the officer interrupts her, "I don't see an imminent danger."

"Listen here now! I'm going to bring my husband's head here and put it right on your desk." Mom demonstrates each move with her arms.

Several middle-aged officers who were doing paperwork at the back of the room now stop and jerk their heads to look at Mom in stunned silence.

Mom turns around and storms out of the building, not even noticing me standing by the door. I run after her and grab her hand. She finally slows down. I can feel the tension in her hand, and it makes me unsettled. What will happen to us now? Dad's addiction will probably never go away. Most likely, he'll never be free of it.

"Do you want soda?" Mom asks me as we pass the grocery shopping area where Kristen and I sold her butter.

"Yes," I reply excitedly. "I want Tarkhun."

We get into line at the closest booth. When it's our turn, the salesperson opens a bottle of green bubbly water, then hands it to me. We continue on our way.

"Maybe I should kill your father?" Mom asks.

Whoa, what? The soda drips out of my mouth and trickles down my chin. The question has chilled me to the bone.

Gathering myself, I weigh and measure my words, then reply in the calmest voice I can master, "No, Mom. The police always find the criminals. You'll go to prison."

She doesn't reply, and we keep walking. Happy that she's dropped the topic, I babble about past episodes of *Simple Maria*.

I'm stunned when Mom says, "Please go to the meadow behind our backyard and look for poisonous mushrooms."

Oh, what should I do now? How do I get out of this? *Lie.*

"OK, I'll go," I say, gulping the last quarter of my soda and giving the empty bottle to Mom.

"Come back through the window," Mom instructs as I take off at a run. "I'll leave the safety bars open for you."

I spring up the hill, take a shortcut through our neighbors' gardens, and skirt around the trees and bushes toward the small meadow. There, I walk in circles, pretending to look for the mushrooms, turning my head right and left, unseeingly staring at the grass. Dad just recently showed me how the poisonous mushrooms look. If only he'd known what Mom would ask of me.

Evening falls soon, and the sky turns dark blue. The moon is bright tonight, blazing in an orangey-yellow hue. I blow my hair away from my eyes and continue theatrically looking right and left, just in case Mom can see me.

As I stroll, the moon keeps moving along with me. I could never understand that. How is it possible? And the moon has human features. It harks back to when I was a baby, and Mom would stand over my crib, looking at me. I'm not sure if I truly remember it or just imagined it.

I stop walking and turn around. I've been here long enough. It'll be believable that I've thoroughly looked for the mushrooms.

As I head back, I pass a tiny building on my right, which is the small accounting company where Dad works as a watchman. I like this place because Dad allows me to bring my friends here to play on days when the company is closed. I have great memories of my time spent here. One time, I had to climb into one of the windows on the second floor because Dad accidentally forgot the keys, and our dog, Doll, was inside.

The sidewalk encircling our apartment building comes into view, and I walk onto it, trying not to step on the trash scattered about it. Why do people throw things out their windows? I can see cigarette butts, boiled macaroni, used syringes, and . . . deflated balloons?

Holding my breath, I continue walking carefully. As I pass our glassy balcony, I glance up and find myself looking into

Dad's eyes. My heart skips a bit. He says nothing, just looks at me with a solemn expression on his face.

My mouth is so dry. I swallow. Does he know something? His expression is unreadable. Suddenly, he smiles at me, and I feel like I could collapse to the ground from the relief.

I wave at him and continue inching toward my bedroom window, then I climb over its sill and jump loudly onto the floor below.

Arranging my face in a gloomy expression, I say, "There were no mushrooms at all, not even the nonpoisonous ones."

I brace myself for a scolding, but it never comes. Mom surprises me by smiling warmly at me. "It's OK, love."

Does she secretly feel relieved I haven't found mushrooms, or does she feel guilty she asked me to do it?

"I was able to bring a Doctorskaya bologna sandwich from work today," she says.

"Great," I say and go to the fridge in the corner of the room.

I put the sandwich on a saucer and take it to my bed. Sitting on its edge, I start to chew.

Mom locks the security bars on the window, her lips moving like she's reminding herself of something. I watch absentmindedly as she draws the curtains, walks around the room doing some chores, and then goes to her bed and lifts the thin mattress.

I gasp. There, on the metal platform of the bed, lie two ancient-looking, long-bladed swords.

"What are those for?" I yelp.

"For protection," she says and covers them back with the mattress. "I have them from my last job."

She starts humming something under her breath, then half sits, half lies in her bed to knit.

"Last job?" I ask her stupidly. Does she mean the one where she worked as a custodian?

"When I worked as President Yeltsin's bodyguard," she answers.

I shake my head. "No, you never worked as a bodyguard."

"Don't give me an argument," she snaps. "I did work as a bodyguard."

I look at her wild gaze; there's a vulnerability there. She wants to be believed.

I nod at her. "You were a bodyguard."

"Yes," she says cheerfully. "I once jumped out of a helicopter with a parachute to save the president's life."

I have an inkling where this fantasy is coming from. She maybe heard the helicopter this afternoon and now is concocting this story on the go.

I pat myself on the back for not arguing with her, but then something inside me protests. I need to say what I really think.

"Mom," I start gently, "you need to go to a doctor. A pseeky . . . psocky . . . psy-chee-a-trist. A psychiatrist."

"I'm not crazy!" Mom screeches. "How dare you! Never say that again."

Still, I go on. "Mom, you mix reality with something else."

"Reality?"

I lower my gaze and bite my lip to keep from saying more, then put the empty saucer down on the floor and get under the blanket.

As I lie there, staring at the ceiling, another question rolls off my tongue. "Where are your parents, Mom?"

She doesn't take even a second to think over her answer. In a loud, high-pitched voice, she says, "They switched me with another couple's infant while traveling on a train."

"What does that mean?"

"It was an accident, but as a result, I was raised by the wrong parents."

Given Mom's answers, I won't ever find out where my grandma and grandpa are—if they're even still alive—or if I have uncles, aunts, and cousins. I sigh, watching Mom skillfully work her knitting needles. In motion, they look like the rotating helicopter blades I saw earlier.

"So where are the parents who raised you?" I ask, trying again.

Mom shrugs. "Minsk, Belarus."

I don't believe that either. Did she abandon her parents maybe? Did they abandon her? Was she raised in an orphanage? Poor Mom.

I saw once on her marriage certificate, which was lying torn-up on the floor after one of her fights with Dad, that she was born in Abkhazia, a small country on the border with Sochi. Does that place have answers? Probably not, as the country had a war recently. I know that because Dad sheltered a family of Georgian refugees from there for a whole year. I smile, recalling the young couple and their toddler son. I liked them. They always shared the hazelnuts with me that they liked to fry. I hope their life is much better now.

"Would you like me to show you how to make an origami crane?" Mom asks, rerouting my thoughts.

"Yes," I reply.

"Come to the table, my sweet baby daughter."

I scurry to the chair on Mom's other side and watch unblinkingly as she tears a piece of paper out of a notebook, folds it diagonally, and presses it along the seam.

"See?" she asks me. "Memorize all the steps."

I doubt I'll remember them. Mom continues skillfully moving her hands, manipulating the paper into different shapes, and I know for a fact I won't remember the steps.

As Mom completes the origami bird, she shows me how to pull on its long tail to set its wings flapping up and down. The bird looks more like a pigeon than a crane.

I take the origami to my bed and put it on my pillow. Lying down next to it, I close my eyes and start imagining I'm someone else. Today, I'll be an eighteen-year-old girl with curly, dark hair and brown eyes, who likes dressing fashionably and wearing high heels. And I'll have a boyfriend similar to the character in the *Amphibian Man* movie. He has superpowers that allow him to breathe underwater and bring me pearls from the bottom of the sea. Most importantly, he keeps me safe.

Good and Bad

Light fills the room. I reluctantly stretch out and sit up. It was a restless night. The squeaky iron bed kept waking me. At least one time, I was glad it did. I had a nightmare about some animal dying. I wish I hadn't remembered that. My mood takes a nosedive. Why do dreams feel so real?

I smell cigarette smoke in the room, which means Mom has just left for work. The smell is pungent. Why do adults often enjoy either smoking or drinking or both? Do some taste buds appear suddenly when you reach a certain age? I hope not.

A knock on our windowpane startles me. I gasp, then freeze with fear. *Who is it? Another pervert?* Probably a bored neighbor walking around the building, wishing to say hi or to chat. My friends also often knock on my window to ask me to come outside.

Before I can open the curtains, I hear a sob, and it makes my ears buzz with anxiety.

I shift the curtain open just an inch and see that it's our taciturn neighbor, whose name I don't even know. Usually he doesn't greet us kids, but now he's here.

"What's wrong?" I ask, opening the curtains wider.

He sighs, blinking his tears away. "Does your dad have a shovel?"

"Yes. But what happened?"

"I . . . I bought discounted beef liver, and it poisoned my dog. Now I don't know how to tell my wife. She won't survive the news. And I don't want her to see Lada dead."

A chill prickles my forearms. *My dream.* Poor Lada was such a pretty Maltese with curly gray fur and amber eyes.

"Was the beef expired?" I ask.

The man pushes his long gray hair aside, then shakes his head. "It was probably infected with something."

His shoulders start shaking. "My wife and I, we don't have kids. Lada was our everything. Oh God, how will I tell her?"

"Maybe you can give her a little puppy?"

He doesn't reply, and another sob escapes his lips.

"I'm going to get the shovel now," I say hastily. "I'll bring it to you in the entrance hall."

"Dad!" I yell, knocking on his door. "Give me a shovel. Our neighbor needs to bury his dog."

Dad opens the door, and after I explain the situation, he goes to the balcony and returns with a big rusty shovel.

"I'll bring it out," he says as I try to reach for it.

When Dad returns, he takes me to his room and points to a small tube on the table. "I thought you'd come yesterday. I bought you a kaleidoscope."

"What is it for?" I ask, lifting the thing up.

"Go outside and look at the sun through it."

In the courtyard, I press my eye to it, raise it up, and see an instant burst of color.

"Twist the rim," a neighbor, Mrs. Melnik, yells from her window on the first floor.

I do, and tiny mosaics inside the tube bounce around, falling out, falling in, and mixing. I want to enjoy my toy, I do, but thoughts of the poor dead dog keep crawling in.

I go to our mailbox and hide the kaleidoscope inside for now, then nod in greeting to Mrs. Zhuk, who's descending the stairs.

Her long dress is brushing against the concrete steps. She's lost so much weight since a tragedy in her family. Her son, or son-in-law—I'm not sure which—drowned several years ago while swimming in the sea at night, drunk. For a year, Mrs. Zhuk stood on her porch, crying. Alcohol is evil; it can kill a person in so many ways.

"Laura," she says, sounding cheerful for a change. "Do you want to help me and the other kids?"

"Yes, of course," I reply. "With what?"

"Everyone's in my garden, trimming the bushes. Go on ahead. Once I check my mail, I'll bring some homemade lemonade."

I run to the garden at the side of the backyard, immediately spotting Ava in the company of three of our neighbor boys, Mark, Paul, and Adam.

"Do you have pruners for me?" I ask them, entering the garden.

"Laura!" yells Ava. "You're here!"

"Where there's food, there's Laura," Mark says sarcastically.

"Shut up," I snap and look at his scratched eyelid. "Are you now holding company with cats?"

He smirks. "No."

"And what do you mean, food?"

"Mrs. Zhuk told us to eat the grapes," Ava says, blowing a curly lock of hair off her forehead.

I look up at the black grapes hanging from wooden frames—they're all swollen with juice, ripe. They're Isabella grapes, the most delicious.

"I rarely see you anymore," I say to Adam.

He laughs. "I spent the summer at my grandparents' place while my parents were training to climb Mount Elbrus."

"Are you for real?"

He nods. "Yes."

"That's why you have no tan and are pale as a ghost. You were away from the beach all summer."

"As if you have a tan."

Ava interrupts us by giving me her pruners. "Here, you can have them."

I cut dead branches off the bushes for the next hour. Somehow, in the end, they start resembling poodles. Very funny.

Our work is done. We finish the pitcher of lemonade, thank Mrs. Zhuk, and go to the woods above the gardens to play.

We have lots of fun. At first, we build secret hideouts, then pretend to be bears and jump out when someone's passing by. We laugh so hard that we cry and cough.

Then, to win a bet, I climb a tree and walk from one of its branches to the branch of another tree, just like Tarzan would do.

"What do you want as your reward?" Ava asks.

"A piece of Love Is gum," I answer. "I'm collecting the wrappers."

As evening nears, Peter and another of our neighbors, Nicholas, join us. Nicholas should have a grudge against me, but he doesn't. When we were six, I threw a stone in one of the gardens surrounding our courtyard and unknowingly hit him in the head. The poor boy had to skip first grade to let his wound heal and his hair grow back.

I hope he doesn't have a scar from the incident. I try to look at the spot, but a mop of dark copper hair hides his scalp completely.

All of us come out of the woods and roam the streets. Something happens to the elastic in Peter's shorts, and they suddenly slide down. Maybe it wouldn't be as funny if he didn't immediately step in animal poop.

Humor intact, Peter laughs louder than all of us, jumps into the grass to clean his shoe, then runs home. If anyone were to see and smell him now, they'd think Peter had pooped in his pants.

When Ava's coiled hair gets tangled in a prickly bush, we don't laugh. We're all afraid of her big brother George, who's very protective of her. After freeing Ava's hair, we allow ourselves to laugh again.

I feel guilty when I remember Lada. I shouldn't have fun. I should go home. Besides, I really need to use the bathroom.

"I'm going home," I say to everyone.

"Why?" Ava asks.

"To pee."

"Do your business behind a tree," Paul offers, smiling with his bunny teeth on show.

"Have you lost your mind?" I ask, glaring at him.

"What? Do you have something we don't?"

I roll my eyes. "Duh!"

"Come back when you're done," Ava says.

"OK," I reply. "I'll bring my dog to show you some tricks she can do. Wait for me in the courtyard."

I run down the narrow brick-lined stairs that lead from the dumpsters straight to our apartment building. After doing my business, I take Mickey and Doll and go back outside.

When everyone's ready, I begin demonstrating all the tricks Doll can do. She can sit, lie down, stand, and give a paw—all on command. Mickey can't do anything.

The grand finale of our performance is Doll's singing. I slowly start humming the melody of a Russian folk song, "Two Merry Geese," and as soon as I hit the high note, Doll raises her head like a wolf and starts to howl.

Our neighbors are watching too, clapping and oohing and aahing. Suddenly, Doll squirms out of my hands and runs into a neighbor's garden. Mickey perks up his ears, opens his mouth to pant, then dashes after his mother. *What's in there?*

I go to the garden's metal fence and tap on it. "Come back, Doll! Mickey!"

Mickey suddenly yelps, and I jump over the fence, trying to catch both dogs. Just like the Russian proverb warns that if you chase two rabbits, you won't catch either one—it takes a while for me to catch Mickey and Doll. What were they chasing? What scared Mickey? Did something bite him?

"Look!" Ava shouts, pointing to a rosebush.

Oh my, there's a hedgehog, fat and gray-spiked. I've never seen a hedgehog before. Its paws are so cute.

"A hedgehog!" everyone around starts yelling. Even the older ladies stand up to take a good look at it. The poor hedgehog is now trying to bury itself in some fallen leaves.

"Please catch it," a neighbor shouts from the window on the third floor, bobbing his long-haired head to the rock music playing in the background of his apartment.

"Why?" Peter asks, popping his gum.

Oh, Peter is back. In new clothes, of course.

"I want to bring my kids downstairs to show it to them," the man explains.

"OK, sir," Peter says and climbs over the fence too.

"Don't hurt the hedgehog," I say.

"Don't hurt my fingers, rather," Peter grumbles and carefully scoops the hedgehog up. "Eww, its nose is wet."

"What did you expect? It's just like a dog's."

Peter looks at Adam. "And its ears are big like yours."

Adam looks at him, horrified. "My ears aren't big."

"The hedgehog's ears aren't big," I retort simultaneously.

We laugh.

Mickey and Doll start trembling, trying to sniff the small animal in Peter's hands. I scoop them up in my arms and take them home. They don't need the stress, and neither does the hedgehog.

Doll's long eyelashes make me jealous. Why does she even need them? To look like a real doll? I look at Mickey and smirk. His paws are princess-pink. Why does he need to be so cute?

As we enter the corridor, Mom opens our bedroom door and sticks her head out. "Would you like to have a meal at a restaurant?"

"Do we have money?" I ask excitedly.

She shakes her head, then whispers conspiratorially, "A man invited me for dinner. I said no at first but then decided that you and I could have our bellies full."

I nod enthusiastically. "Who is he?"

"Do you remember my friend from Tuapsinskaya?"

"But she's a woman."

Mom laughs. "Yes, the man is her boss."

"Oh, he's rich then."

"Most likely, so order whatever you want and dress in something presentable."

I scan the clothes Mom is wearing. Her suit almost resembles a silver space suit. I've never seen it before. Did she spend her salary shopping for clothes?

"Will you wear high heels?" I ask her hopefully.

Mom scrunches her nose in disgust. "No."

I sigh with disappointment and go to my wardrobe, choosing the same outfit I wore on the first day of the toy store adventure. *The adventure before the misadventure.* For my shoes, I choose Polina and Olivia's pink rubber slippers. They look like they were created for ballet dancing.

The restaurant we walk to is called Cascade and is just five minutes away from home. We arrive quickly. I stare longingly at the adjacent Alenka cafeteria. I'd rather have gone there. They sell cakes and desserts.

When we enter the restaurant, I suddenly feel shy, following Mom closely as she heads to the table where a man with salt-and-pepper hair is sitting. Judging by his reaction, he wasn't expecting me. It's brief, but I catch it.

The man stands up to greet us as we approach. I don't want to look into his hawkish eyes, so I concentrate on his buzz-cut hair. How can it be almost gray when his stubble is still bright brown?

"What wine would you like, Talia?" he asks my mom.

"Feeelix," she says, stretching the word. "I never drink."

Felix bobs his head respectfully and drops the topic.

We sit at the table and turn to look at the waiter walking toward us. The young man with piercing eyes is wearing a ridiculously long white apron that almost reaches his knees. I read the handwritten name tag on his shirt. It says, "Edward." After handing menus to us, Edward walks out of our earshot to stand poised, looking at us.

Before I open my menu, I think of what Mom just told Felix. It's true that she never drinks alcohol. What's the sense in making a fool of yourself? I saw Mom drink only once, and afterward, she was giggling and dancing—dancing stupidly like . . . like she was crazy.

My mother doesn't waste time and calls for the waiter right away. She orders a baked chicken with mushrooms and marinated vegetables, then looks expectantly at me. I hastily choose eggs with red caviar and a cheese-filled pie, feeling greedy but ignoring my inner voice. It's expensive, but I've never tried caviar before.

While the food is being prepared, I go to a row of fountains inside the building. They're cascading, just like the name of the restaurant suggests, with the water smelling like cilantro.

I imagine myself living in a castle with such fountains, walking around them day and night. Only my fountains won't smell of cilantro, of course. They will smell of roses, the dark red roses Mom sometimes uses to make tea.

The shoes on my feet start to hurt my toes. They're too tight. I squeeze my feet and return to the table.

The waiter brings our food, and we start eating. Felix still tries to talk to Mom, but she's too busy enjoying the chicken on her plate. I close my eyes and lick the caviar from the egg halves, one by one. Delicious, salty, and smelling of a mountain river. What would it be like to have enough money to eat like this daily? Would I enjoy the food the same way, or would it turn bland with time?

"No one will snatch the pie from you," Felix chides me, chuckling.

I look at what he's eating. The famous Olivier salad and small fried fish. Red mullet?

"Should we take Laura home?" he asks Mom after the waiter carries our empty plates away.

Mom coughs before answering. "She and I will go home together now, as I need to wake at 4 a.m. tomorrow."

The man's eyebrows shoot up in surprise. But wait, what did he expect?

"Thank you so much for dinner," Mom says, getting up from the table and putting her hand to her heart in gratitude.

I follow her as she slowly backs away, then the both of us walk out through the round entrance of the restaurant and step into the street, which is bustling with listlessly wandering tourists.

"I'll never do that again," Mom says.

"Do what?" I ask.

"Eat on someone else's dime."

I nod understandingly. *I shouldn't have ordered that caviar.*

"Let's walk faster," Mom says. "The dark is dangerous."

"How so?" I ask. I hang out in the dark outside all the time.

"Bad people hide in it."

"I guess you're right." *But bad people hide in the light too.*

We stroll in silence down the alley stairs at the side of the high road, then through the underpass and up our street. When we come to our apartment building, I remember the kaleidoscope.

"Look what Dad bought me," I say, rolling it out of the mailbox.

"This is amazing, Laura," Mom says, then mumbles under her breath, "A wonderful father and a horrible husband."

"You know what it is?" I ask, shifting the topic back to the kaleidoscope.

"No, he didn't!" Mom suddenly yelps, entering the corridor of our apartment.

"What?" I ask, alarmed.

"Victor painted the kitchen without asking me."

"So? It's a pinkish beige, very pretty."

Mom hums in disapproval, then motions for me to follow her into our bedroom and locks the door.

"Victor!" she yells. "You're an asshole! How dare you paint the walls without my permission!"

I cover my ears with the palms of my hands and watch Mom's mouth get foamy at the corners as she continues shouting at him. What's this foam? Is Mom ill?

After a surprisingly long silence, Dad answers, "Who do you think you are, bitch?"

Feeling limp, I sink to the floor and start playing with my kaleidoscope, looking at our chandelier through it. And now time to play with my Barbie. Will I ever grow up to be a young woman like her? Or will I die before that? Sometimes it seems to me I'm not important and won't live beyond nineteen years old. Other times it seems the entire world revolves just around me, and all the people on this earth, including the president, are fakes.

I was so absorbed in my thinking that I didn't notice when Mom calmed down. Her expression is serene as she sits in her armchair, knitting a sweater with four knitting needles. Four needles! How skillful she is.

I look at her for a while, and her calmness calms me too.

"Maybe you and Dad can divide the apartment in two parts," I offer. "Then you can build a front door in place of our window, or Dad can build a door on the glass balcony."

"Great idea," Mom says and looks at the window, imagining it as a door, I think.

I get up and sit in her lap, watching as she resumes her knitting. No wonder the process calms her—it's like listening to a pleasant, ever-constant rhythm.

Mom kisses my nose. "You're heavy, you know?"

I giggle and slide to the floor again, then crawl to the fridge and open it to see what I can have for breakfast tomorrow. It's empty.

"Pity we almost never have food," I say, closing the small fridge door.

"What are you talking about?" Mom asks sharply. "I cooked buckets of bologna salad in the past. Our fridge was cracking from the loads of food."

I look at her sideways. Is she fantasizing again? Only one time was our fridge full when Dad was renting our spare room to tourists, who then asked Mom to store their food in our fridge. I remember sitting in front of it, staring at the food inside, dreaming of cutting just one little slice of the smoked cheese or the bologna sausage.

I go lie down in my bed, turn to the wall, and try to fall asleep. I'm still so full from dinner that my stomach hurts, and it makes me feel sad for some reason. The memories of the poor dead dog come in a whoosh, and I feel like crying. Why couldn't life be made of only good parts? Why is it always good and bad, then good and bad again?

Chapter Eleven
Mother's Intuition

Bright light wakes me up the next morning. The rays are piercing our room through the orange curtains and two edges of the window. I get up and peek outside. The grass on the lawn is gleaming in the sunlight. It's very good weather for a day at the beach. I haven't been there for two weeks. I'd better go today.

In a rush, I get dressed, slip on my flip-flops, and, neglecting to brush my hair or teeth, run outside. An oh-so-wonderful day is waiting for me.

"Where are you going?" Kristen shouts from her balcony.

I smile at her familiar musical voice. "To the beach. Wanna come with me?"

"I can't. My dad is coming to see me today."

Oh, right, her parents are divorced. That's why she lives with only her mom and likes to talk to our male neighbors. She even asked one of them if he wanted to be her daddy. So sad. I can't imagine living without my dad.

"Enjoy your day," I shout and continue on my way up the driveway and down the street.

I come across a homeless-looking man with a dozen bags strung around his shoulders. I slow down to let him pass me, but he pauses and gestures with his arm for me to continue going.

"Show me the way to that church, girl," he says, pointing into the distance and aiming his long nose in the same direction.

I look and see the golden domes of the Cathedral of the Archangel Michael. I know how to get there, but I don't want to walk with this stranger.

"Come on," he orders me authoritatively. "Go, and I'll follow you."

I don't want to.

"Come on!" he repeats.

Reluctantly, I start walking. When the man stops to ask a passerby for directions, I slowly back away, then run to the harbor square at the end of the street.

"Did you forget to brush your hair?" a teenage girl asks when I stop at a crosswalk traffic light.

I press my hand to my rumpled hair and rake it with my fingers. Well, if I had nails as long as this girl's, I wouldn't need a brush. They're red, sharp, and obviously fake. I widen my eyes at them, pretending to be appalled. It works, and the girl steps away with a nervous giggle.

The light changes to green, and I hurry to cross the road ahead of the girl. That's when I see Matilda in the crowd on the other side.

"Matilda!" I yell.

Matilda is my childhood friend—well, not exactly my friend, more like my babysitter. She's ten years older than me, and when she lived one floor above us, she volunteered to babysit me. I think she liked pretending to be my mother.

I launch myself at her, jumping over the few feet between us. How could I not recognize her when I scanned the crowd earlier? She's the tallest young lady I know, and her hair is fire-engine red.

I loop my hands around her neck and jump up and down with joy. "Finally, you returned from Moscow."

She puts her beautifully tanned arms around me and says, "You look perfect. I'm going to take you to the Russian Institute of Theater Arts in Moscow when you grow up, and you'll become an actress."

Excitement catches in my throat. I'm thrilled to pieces. *Me, an actress?* I know Matilda has starred in at least one movie so far. Would I be able to memorize all the lines for my roles? I'd rather go to some university for dancers in Moscow.

"Do you wanna go with me to the beach?" I ask.

"I'm just returning from there," she says. "Do you like swimming?"

"Yes, and I like doing acrobatics in the water. If only I didn't have to get wet. I don't like that."

"You're too funny," she says and looks at the traffic lights. "I'll be on my way now, but I'll come visit you."

"Will you bring Layla with you?"

Layla is Matilda's best friend, a very attractive young woman with eyes shaped like a cat's. I sometimes think that if I stare at her long enough, her beauty will somehow rub off on me. But I keep away from her family now because her dad's stares make me uncomfortable.

"Layla and I aren't friends anymore," Matilda replies.

I nod as if understanding, then say, "Layla is our second neighbor to get a car. She also has an iron garage on the hill below our courtyard. Are you planning on buying a car?"

"Not yet. Don't tell my parents, but I spend a lot of my money on parties."

"'Parties?'"

"Discotheques. My friends and I go there to dance, drink, and have fun."

Drink? I look at her in horror, immediately thinking of my dad.

"Don't drink, please," I say.

She laughs uproariously, shakes her wild hair, and walks into the crosswalk. I notice a young man with a bag slung over his shoulder on the other side of the road. He's not moving, just looking at Matilda unblinkingly. *Is he smitten?* I smile at my romantic imaginings and turn away.

As I stroll past the seaport, I feel like I'm already missing Matilda, and I wonder how it's possible that we sometimes come across people who are important to us just by coincidence.

I saunter across the harbor square and toward the promenade. So many mouthwatering smells are coming from the surrounding food stands. Unbearably delicious. The vendors are selling everything from hamburgers to salty corn on the cob. My dad and I once sold crayfish here, but the neighbors started complaining about the smells when we boiled it.

How can I find money right now so I can buy something to snack on? When I was little, I would walk around, asking passersby for a coin or two for ice cream. Maybe I can try the same thing now?

I scan the crowd surreptitiously, searching for a kind face. *That full-figured woman walking with her little white poodle looks kind.* Dog people, as a rule, are always kind. Yes, I'll ask her.

I take a deep breath for courage and call to her, "Excuse me, ma'am! Could you please give me some money to buy an ice cream cone?"

"Sure, girl," she replies cheerfully, reaching for her purse.

I pull at my clothes awkwardly, feeling suddenly shy. Then, to hide my face from the woman, I squat to stroke the fluffy fur of her cute dog.

"Here you go," she says, slipping a bill into my hand.

"Thank you, thank you," I say, straightening up.

As she leaves, I walk to the side of the promenade, away from the torrent of people, and look at the bill in my hand. It's a big one, 200 rubles. I can already buy something but why stop? I can earn more.

I look for another kind face in the crowd but get distracted by a man walking with a white cane for blind people. He's tapping it against the pavement slabs to make sure it's safe for him to walk. I step away politely to let him pass, but he suddenly changes direction and sticks his cane right into my foot.

I jump away, sidestepping him, making even more room for him, but he changes direction again and sticks his cane into my foot once more. I run away. The man tries to catch up with me for a few seconds, then continues on his way. Was he poking fun at me? I stare at his back incredulously. He isn't doing it to anyone else.

I return to my task and look for kind faces. There's a woman buying nesting matryoshka dolls in a souvenir shop, but when she turns, I see that she's a teenager. I look at another woman who's drinking a strawberry milkshake, walking to the beach with wet hair. It's a bit late to run after her. There's also a young couple jogging, but they are too busy talking to each other.

Now the closest person with a kind face is a man playing at the shooting stand on my left. He seems like a father type. I approach him.

"Excuse me, sir," I say. "C-could you give me some money for ice cream?"

"I'm not carrying any money on me," he answers, not even turning to look at me. *Then how did you pay for the game?*

The refusal stinging, I step away with embarrassment.

"Careful!" the worker from the shooting stand rasps in a barely audible, gruff voice. There's something in his neck—a tube for breathing?

"Careful!" he wheezes out again. *Careful of what?*

Before I can look around, I hear a bicycle honking on my left. I jump aside, relieved I wasn't hit. My heart is pounding now, and I feel my ears burning. The hit wouldn't have been dangerous, but the near miss reminds me of the time I was almost struck by a train.

I was walking along the railroad track one day when I started hearing the blaring of a train whistle. I was sure it was coming from the woods on my right. When the honking grew louder and more frantic, I looked back and, to my utter shock, saw that it was right behind me. I had only a few seconds to jump away.

My thoughts return to my money project. Ahead of me is a couple in their sixties, walking hand in hand, clad in only their swimsuits. Mom said it's rude to walk on the promenade in your swimsuit, and now I see what she meant. But the couple is probably kind because chances are they have grandkids.

I march toward them. "I'm sorry. Would you mind giving me some money for ice cream?"

The man and woman stop and tilt their heads at me simultaneously.

"Shameful," the man says, lowering his furry gray brows in disapproval.

"Where are your parents?" his wife asks in a milder voice.

"I mistook you for my aunt and uncle," I lie, stepping out of their way.

I pretend to head toward a group of adults sitting on a bench. I hope the couple will believe me. The last thing I need is for them to think I'm a lost child and call the police. It happened to me once already.

When the couple disappears from view, I give begging one last chance. It isn't easy after all.

This time I'll choose a person who doesn't look kind to see if that works better. I spot such a person immediately. Dressed in a short black dress with a golden belt circling her waist, the woman is walking along the promenade quickly, her lips set in a thin line of determination.

"Excuse me, miss!" I address her shyly while trying to catch up with her long strides. "Could you please give me—"

"Get lost," she cuts me off and continues walking, skipping the pavement in yard-long steps.

I swallow the hurt. Being a beggar isn't my thing. I look at the money I already have. *Thank you, kind lady.*

I turn around and go to the food vendor I saw earlier. After buying a fried bun with potato filling, I buy a bottle of Fanta in a shop nearby and slowly head for my favorite beach, Morisa Toreza.

The hot bun tastes divine. I don't want the eating to end, but it does. I start drinking the Fanta, its bubbles tickling my nose. I wish for it to be sweeter, but it's more like sour.

By the time I reach the beach, I feel electrified with energy and ready to swim like a champ. I choose an empty spot on the rocks and put my clothes there in a neat pile.

Two cute, chubby toddlers are playing on the pebbles on the shore, fighting over the shovel they have. I want to tell them to take turns and be fair, but then I look at my cotton panties and decide not to attract attention to me not having a swimsuit. It's so embarrassing, but I didn't want Mom spending money on it. Next year, though, when my body starts growing like other eleven-year-old girls' bodies, I'll have to buy a two-piece swimsuit or stay home.

I look around, make sure no one's watching, and hurry to the water, then wade through it. The coolness reaches my waist. I take a deep breath and plunge under the water, swimming quickly to warm myself up. When I can't stand holding my breath anymore, I slowly breathe out bubbles of air while floating to the surface.

I continue swimming in rhythm with the tidal ripples. When I reach the end of the wave-breaking seawall on my right, I gingerly grab its edge and start clambering up, trying not to think of the scary creatures living here, like dark crabs and anything else that my imagination can conjure.

Safely on top of the seawall, I straighten up and walk along it like it's a runway. I imagine myself as Cindy Crawford, a top model. I look unseeingly straight ahead with all the haughtiness I can muster.

At the highest point of the seawall, I stop and prepare to dive in. First, I take a few steps back, then run forward and jump into the air. So exhilarating! I roll into a somersault and begin to count my rotations—one, two . . . *ouch!* Only one and a half rotations. Instead of diving in, I belly-flopped onto the water. It felt like a concrete floor.

I grit my teeth in pain and sink to the sea floor. As my toes touch the rocks, I bounce off them and swim back up. I start worrying that I'll run out of air in my lungs before I reach the surface. I didn't know it was that deep here; it's probably ten feet or more.

Thankfully, I start seeing the light through the top layer of water above me. I paddle my arms faster and slide into the purifying, seaweed-smelling air.

My breath recovers quickly, and I swim toward a buoy, where I take a minute to enjoy the view. Shiny blue seawater, small ships in the distance, and flocks of seagulls above. The coastline is quite far from this point.

Suddenly, all those movies I watched about sharks and sea snakes start getting to me, making me terrified that something might touch my leg now. I look at the sky and try to shut down my imagination. The Black Sea is safe—no dangerous sharks here, no snakes, no other biting creatures, only harmless fish and, from time to time, some barely venomous jellyfish.

I flop over on my back and try to relax, floating on the gentle waves. Warm and nice. I can even close my eyes.

Am I really sure there are no creatures crawling on the buoy? No hidden sharp objects? No nets or traps? Time to swim back to land, where it's much safer.

I launch my body forward, rocketing toward the shore, kicking my legs hard, pushing the water out of my way with my arms, and soon my toes brush against the pebbles. Water is rarely shallow so far from the shore, but maybe this beach is different. I can walk the rest of the way.

It's a funny feeling when you trudge in the water as though you're dressed in a very heavy, long dress. I start dancing. It makes my movement fluid like . . . well, like water.

Suddenly, the ground under me disappears, and I fall under the water. I try to fight my way back, but my lungs have no air, and my body feels heavy, like it's filled with stones. I push and push myself upward, but it's no use. My mind goes fuzzy.

Walk, Laura, walk. Some inner voice is talking to me. My brain? My subconscious? God? I gather my last ounce of strength and walk forward. One step, two, three, and my head pops out of the water. What a relief!

I gulp in a few breaths, then start to breathe normally. It's a wonderful sensation to be able to breathe freely. *Thank you, God; thank you for saving me!*

As I start swimming to the shore, I look ahead and see my mother strolling toward the shore. What a coincidence that of all the spots on the beach, she chose this one—and even that she's at the beach in the first place. She's obviously oblivious to the fact I'm right in front of her in the water.

Mom's eyes widen as she sees me, and she gives me one of her rare huge smiles. I hobble onto the shore and run into her outstretched arms. When I was underwater, I thought I'd never see her again. Only once before have I experienced something that scary while swimming. That time, a wave hit me from behind, then rolled me with the pebbles and, thankfully, threw me onto the shore, safe and sound.

"I didn't know you were here," Mom says.

"I didn't know you were here," I say and quickly bend to dress. "Didn't you leave for work this morning?"

She sighs. "I forgot my bus pass, and the driver kicked me out at the next bus stop."

"What a gentleman," I huff.

"A jerk. I cried. But I'm making the best of my day. I even visited an acquaintance that lived in that area."

I nod, getting distracted by music blasting from a nearby café. The voices singing are dreamlike and magical, reverberating in the space in layers of sound. I recognize only the word *heart* in English but try to memorize the others.

"It's the band Modern Talking," Mom says, noticing my fascination.

I rock from side to side while she pulls off her clothes and piles them on the rocks. Her swimsuit is blue, decorated with big bows.

"Should I wait for you?" I ask, noticing she brought a towel to bask in the sun later.

"No, go home," she replies.

Something shiny on the wet pebbles attracts my attention. A seashell? A tide of foamy seawater threatens to roll it back into the sea, and I run to grab it. I stare at it in disbelief. It's a wide, golden semicircle—an earring.

I return to Mom and hand it to her.

She examines the earring at length, turning it from side to side and reading the hallmark.

"It's fourteen-karat," she declares. "Great quality."

I peep around. There are hundreds of people on the beach. No way we'd be able to find the owner. For all we know, the earring could've been in the sea for years.

"Could it have traveled from another city?" I ask.

"Even from another country," Mom suggests.

"What will we do with it? You can't wear it without its mate."

"I'll pawn it for some money."

"Great idea."

Now I know why some people walk along the shoreline with metal detectors. I make a mental note to search for gold in the fall when there are no tourists on the beaches.

Quite happy with myself for finding the treasure, I ruffle my hair with my fingers and then stand, watching the sea and waiting for Mom to go into the water.

"Do you see that horizon line?" I ask her, pointing to the distance.

"Yes, of course," she replies.

"It's where the earth starts curving down."

"Nonsense. The earth is flat."

Startled, I blink, then gaze at her. A giggle escapes my lips. Oops, I didn't mean to laugh at my mother, and I shouldn't argue. This is another wacky thing she believes in. She once argued with a pediatrician that my lice weren't lice but ticks. If the doctor couldn't change her mind about simple facts, I have no chance either.

When Mom tiptoes toward the edge of the sea, and the waves start dashing against her ankles, I head home, feeling ridiculously tired and unsteady on my feet. And hungry again. All that sun and swimming . . .

I rush to the refrigerator once I'm back in the apartment. Nothing is there, still. No magic. I go to the kitchen and make super sweet tea. After drinking it, I return to the room and lie in bed for a nap.

In my dream, I see myself sitting on a hill, staring longingly at tall, flashy buildings on the other side of a dark river. What's this beautiful city that shines like tiny diamonds?

Waking up, I yawn contentedly and slide out of bed to play on the floor. I take some red plaid scraps of fabric my mother gave me and start sewing a long, flared skirt for my Barbie.

I jump with a start at a loud knock on our front door. I go open it, and holy smokes, there's a buck-naked man standing in the entrance hall.

"Please call for an adult!" he begs, desperately trying to twist his body away from my view. I only look at his long black hair.

"Dad!" I yell, but he's already rushing to the front door.

I leave, although curiosity is eating me alive. Was this man locked out of his apartment? Or kicked out? By his lover? By his lover's husband? My lips twitch in amusement.

I sit back on the floor and pick the threaded needle back up, continuing stitching Barbie's skirt. A little while later, my curiosity gets the better of me, and I open the door a crack to peek into Dad's room.

The man is sitting in an armchair, fully dressed in Dad's clothes. He's gesticulating wildly, telling my father something while his Adam's apple is jumping comically in his thin neck. He still seems relaxed, not agitated the way he was in the entrance hall.

Dad catches my gaze, and I close my door. In the few seconds I looked, I noticed one more thing: the utter compassion in Dad's eyes. I'm always amazed by his kindness.

I sit down on my bed and leaf through one of my picture books. This one shows a lot of snow that we rarely have in Sochi. I don't like the cold, but the pictures make me want to spend an evening running with my friends in the courtyard while brushing the shining snow off the palm trees.

I turn back to page one and start to read. Half an hour later, I hear the front door open and then shut. I get up and run to Dad.

"Who was that stranger?" I ask.

"Do you need a name?" Dad asks rhetorically, and from his tone, I know he's not going to give me any explanations.

"Haven't you noticed anything?" Dad asks.

I look at him quizzically, then scan the room and gasp. In the corner, on a thin blanket on the floor, lie hundreds of bananas. My knees buckle. *How?*

Dad senses my question. "I found them thrown in a dumpster behind a convenience store."

"But they're perfect!" I exclaim.

"I agree. Just some overripe spots here and there."

I rush to the pile and kneel in front of it. I'm not sure I've ever tasted bananas before, as they're the most expensive fruit on the market. I should make a wish before I eat the first one. *OK, I wish Dad would stop drinking.* I look at Dad guiltily and pick up a banana.

"Peel it like this," he says, pantomiming the movements.

I close my eyes and chew my first-ever bite. Maybe it's not as sweet as desserts and not as thirst-quenching as watermelons, but it's fulfilling. I quickly finish one and then eat another.

"Don't overdo it," Dad says as I pick up a third banana. "You don't want to spend the night before school on the toilet."

He laughs at his own joke, but I don't. My appetite instantly vanishes. The mention of school makes me feel sick. It starts tomorrow. I'll have to see my cruel classmates who—

I can't finish my thought, because Dad asks, "Can I sell some bananas to our neighbors?"

"No," I reply adamantly.

"Why not?"

"Having so much of something makes me happy."

"But we'll earn money and buy something else."

Yeah, right. You'll buy vodka.

"If you wish," I say and get up. "I'm going to the courtyard."

"Be safe."

Outside, I walk across the lawn, looking for fireflies. The start of the evening is their favorite time, but they're not here.

Maybe it's not their favorite part of the summer. I change direction and go sit on the street stairs.

I place my palms under my chin and watch the bustling city below. A sense of helpless sadness washes over me. The summer break is over now. It's the last day of August 1993. What will happen to us in the future? Something good? Something bad? Or, as always, good and bad?

Back to School

My alarm clock goes off early because it's a school day. I scramble out of bed and shuffle over to the open window to look outside. The leaves on a maple tree have turned golden, as if nature is aware that fall is coming. I breathe in the fresh morning air and think of the dream I had that I still vividly remember. In it, my mom was shouting at me while her hair grew darker and darker, and mice were skittering about. I shudder at the images. What could it mean?

I place my hands on the window glass and push myself off it, then go to the kitchen. Mickey is sleeping on a chair, curled up in a big furry ball. I prop my foot on the bottom rung of the chair and caress Mickey's head, then move to the cabinets to search for flour.

The sight of a nearly empty bag makes me unsettled as a memory arises. One night I was so hungry, I woke up from the pain in my stomach and asked Mom to give me our last bit of flour. She'd suggested waiting until morning, but I wasn't able to fall asleep, so I guiltily took the flour and fried myself pancakes in the middle of the night.

Again, with a guilty conscience, I take the last bit of flour, mix it with water and sugar, then start frying pancakes. I give one to Mickey, and he sucks it down almost without chewing, then hungrily watches me eat mine.

"No, not giving you anything, you sweet tooth," I say.

Mickey rolls his eyes and goes back to sleep. It scares me for a second, as I think he may have another epileptic episode, but no, he's truly dozing and perfectly fine. Even snoring.

I hurry to my wardrobe and rummage through my things, finding my school uniform at the very back. Being too lazy to take my nightgown off, I pull my uniform right over it, then grab my new blue school satchel and dart outside.

My school is in easy walking distance. Soon enough I enter its yard. Students from all grades, first to eleventh, have already gathered here, waiting for the celebratory concert to start. The start of the school year is a very big holiday; it even has a name—Knowledge Day.

I gingerly line up with my fifth-grade class, gritting my teeth in fear that someone will come to torment me. They don't. I look sideways. All the girls but me have big white bows on their heads and are holding flowers for our new homeroom teacher. Maybe later I can ask my neighbor Mrs. Belaya, who's a teacher too, for a bouquet. She brings at least thirty of them home each year after the first-day-of-school celebrations. Meanwhile, I hope our homeroom teacher won't like me less than the others because I don't have a gift for her.

The concert starts at 8 a.m., and a high school student marches across the schoolyard with a first grader on his shoulder, a cute little girl with blue eyes and black eyelashes. She's ringing a huge silver bell with all the strength she's got. Several groups of schoolchildren follow the pair around the yard. Then the other entertainments start: dancing, singing, reciting poetry—a little bit of everything.

The principal follows this up with a formal speech, then gestures for us to go inside the school building.

We all file through the wide entrance door, and I go to the second floor, to our new classroom. I gaze at my new homeroom teacher. She looks like a strong woman, with short hair and shrewd eyes.

"As you already know," she says when we take our seats, "I'm Mrs. Almaz. I'm your new homeroom teacher, and I'll also be your English-as-a-foreign-language teacher."

"Awesome," everyone shouts.

"You'll start studying English for the first time, and I congratulate you on this! This language will open new worlds for you."

Everyone starts clapping excitedly, and most of the girls jump up from their seats and run to hug the teacher. Such suck-ups. Watching them makes me sick, or maybe I'm jealous. No teacher would want me to hug them. I'm unlikable. I don't have nicely ironed clothes or glossy shoes, and I don't have beautifully styled hair.

My previous teacher never hugged me. One time she was giving the other girls candies, and when I got the courage to ask her for one, she lied that she didn't have any left. All the while, the iridescent candies were sticking out of her purse.

I dismiss the memory as irrelevant and focus on examining the lines in my palms. I'll never have to be in the same room as my previous teacher again.

There are no real lessons today. We listen to the rules we'll have to abide by in middle school, then take textbooks for each subject and leave the classroom. Holding my school satchel, I quickly head toward the exit. I won't let the bullies catch up with me today. Or any day, for that matter.

Keeping my speed up, I get to the courtyard back home in no time. The neighborhood ladies are sitting on the bench, nibbling on sunflower seeds, all coincidentally dressed in purple. They wave for me to come to them, probably curious about my first day in school this year. But no, it turns out they just want me to go to the store and buy them loaves of fresh bread.

"Use the change to buy yourself ice cream," Mrs. Zima says, handing me a pile of money. She's as kind as ever; even stray cats follow her around because of that. I once saw a dozen cats waiting at her front door for her to feed them.

"Put the money in your pocket so you don't lose it," she tells me.

Delighted, I leave my school satchel under the bench and run down the hill. Right when I'm in the middle of the main road, Murphy's law strikes, and my forward lean turns into a fall. I land face down on the asphalt. *What an idiot!*

Tires screech. Horns honk. I squeeze my eyes shut and brace myself for a hit. When nothing happens, I open one eye and peek around. The traffic has completely stopped. I spring back to my feet and race to the curb. *Why do I always embarrass myself?*

"Well, well, if it isn't Shura," a voice taunts me, and I recognize it as George's, Ava's brother.

"Don't call me Shura," I snap, finding him among other passersby. "I'm Laura now!"

I look at the tennis racket in his hand. He's probably returning from tennis practice at Riviera Park.

"What, dreaming of becoming a champion?" I ask.

He ignores my jab. "You should have your boy's name back. It fits you better."

"Scumbag!" I almost yell.

"Being rude is wrong, kids," a passerby rebukes, tutting disapprovingly.

He is holding a black briefcase. A lawyer going to the courthouse? I wait for him to cross the road, shoot my gaze skyward, then look back at George and stick my tongue out at him.

"You're an eyesore," he comments.

I snort and move on, going about my business. When in the supermarket, I buy four loaves of bread and select an ice cream called Eskimo for myself. The thin layer of dark chocolate on the ice cream tastes amazing. I walk back slowly, concentrating on the crunchy pieces. Before I know it, I'm back in my courtyard.

"Here," I say, handing the bag to Mrs. Zima and licking the last melted drops from the stick.

Suddenly, two girls jump out of the bushes and startle me. It's Olivia and Polina. I do get really startled and stumble backward, nearly jumping out of my skin. They laugh and scream with delight at my overreaction. In an effort to be a good sport, I start laughing too.

"Let's go play in the backyard," Polina says.

I drop the ice cream stick in my satchel and follow the girls behind the apartment building, where they show me their new red bicycle.

"Wow," I say, sighing. "Will you teach me to ride it?"

"Climb on," Polina offers.

She holds the bike from the back, and Olivia goes to the front and holds the handlebars. Even with all their help, the only thing I'm able to do is sit on it. When I try to pedal, the bike sways left and right, and I become like a tumbler toy. I hear laughter and see some small kids watching us from their windows.

I give up and stand aside to watch the girls take turns circling the backyard effortlessly.

I might as well go home. Waving goodbye, I head for my apartment. There, I decide to take a bath. After that, I'll study my new textbooks, then practice dancing, then take my dogs for a walk. Maybe I'll even pick fruit from trees and make a sweet salad. What a busy bee I'll be!

Chapter Thirteen
A Spy

My first days of school go surprisingly well; no bullies bother me at all. They don't stalk me after classes like they used to. Maybe what's helping is that I've been either running home quickly or taking a different route each day. I'm so glad because I want to study well and become a teacher. I need to catch up on so much of the school program I've missed in the previous three years.

Today, in our English class with Mrs. Almaz, we're studying greetings, introductions, and polite words. I stare at her, feeling jealous that I can't be in her place. I'm going to learn everything in my English textbook and find a library where I can check out an English-Russian dictionary.

The lesson ends too soon. I scribble down my homework assignment and hurry to the next classroom. Even in school, I have to move quickly to avoid my classmates.

I drop my school satchel at my desk and walk to the safety of the crowd in the vast hall. I tiptoe listlessly, back and forth, like on a tightrope, counting silently the wooden boards in the floor. It's a good way to kill time until class starts. The mindless task is soothing.

"Oh, you're beautiful," a woman standing by the window says, sounding surprised.

Startled out of my trance, I glance up at her. Did she just say what I think she said? Did she call me beautiful? *Me?*

I keep staring at her with my mouth hanging open. She has long, silky black hair shining in the sunlight streaming through the window behind her. Maybe she finds me pretty because she looks so different from me?

She smiles at me widely, then her gaze falls down to my worn-out shoes, and she says, "On Monday I'll bring you a pair of new shoes. What class are you in?"

I hesitate before answering. My classmates will laugh at me endlessly if they see me getting a handout. But I can't *not* answer, because it would be rude. My only option is to answer now and then skip school on Monday.

"Five V," I answer reluctantly.

"And where's your classroom?" she asks.

I point toward the corner of the hall. "On the left from the principal's office."

"I won't forget that. And what's your name?"

"Laura. Laura Meer."

A squealing girl runs suddenly out of one of the classrooms and slams into the woman's legs. They both laugh and hug each other. I see that both of them have the same black hair and dark brown eyes. Mother and daughter, I guess.

While the two of them are talking, I take advantage of the interruption to slip back into my classroom. My body feels lighter somehow; I'm in high spirits. All I'm going to think of today is the lady in the hall and what she told me.

When classes are over, I shove my books into my satchel and hurry to the staircase. Jumping onto the banister, I slide down. Yes, I feel like I can soar today. With a cluster of other kids, I slowly cross the schoolyard and go home.

Everything seems brighter today. How come I've never noticed how yellow the flower bushes growing along the lane are? And those green burdock leaves—I've been walking this path every day and haven't seen them at all.

I turn left to the shortcut leading through the woods straight to my driveway. I take exaggerated steps, listening to the rustling foliage. Why haven't I ever noticed how hypnotic this sound is? And the smell . . . mmm. Someone is barbecuing close by. What a wonderful day!

Suddenly, my neck prickles in apprehension. I look around frantically. There's no one, but just in case, I hasten my pace. Then I hear it—the unmistakable buzz of my classmates' voices.

"Hey, you penniless bum!" Lucy, the leader of the pack, shouts. "Do us a favor and leave our school."

I turn and see eight of my classmates turning onto my shortcut path. They stop about a dozen feet away from me. Trying to be intimidating, they line up with their legs apart. I cringe in fear. How stupid it was of me to relax my guard and walk slowly.

"You're so ugly," Lucy adds another insult.

I'm ugly again. Not beautiful.

"Leave me alone," I beg, looking everyone in the eyes.

They laugh, and Lucy's sickly pale face breaks into the coldest smile I've ever seen. If only the teachers knew—Lucy has a dark side.

"Please," I beg again in a ragged gasp.

"Such trash," she growls. "Breathing the same air as you is gross."

I want to say, "Then don't," but I'm afraid of her. I'm afraid of everyone.

"Please!" I moan.

"Pleeeease," another girl, Kate, mocks me in her small, gritty voice. "This stupid butthead is asking for mercy."

How could her soulful baby blue eyes be so deceitful?

Everyone starts walking toward me, and I hide my shaking hands behind my back.

"My dad is coming here to meet me," I lie, trying to sound confident.

For a few seconds, it works, and everyone hesitates, looking around with uncertainty, but then they dismiss my lie.

"That old drunk?" Lucy asks.

"I've been to their house," a third girl, Sarah, tells everyone. "It smelled like an ashtray."

How could Sarah do this to me? She used to be my friend. *Maybe she was never truly my friend.* She hung out with me because I promised to give her an expensive doll—a lie; I never had it. When she realized the truth, she dumped me. What would this popular, pretty girl want to do with me?

"Why are you staring at me like that, dummy?" Sarah asks. "Your eyes are about to pop out. Take a picture. It'll last longer."

I lower my gaze and don't say anything. I'm the most cowardly person in the world. I can't utter a word in my defense. I despise this in myself with all my heart. But . . . I just don't want to get physically hurt.

My silence only makes everyone laugh and insult me more. Am I some kind of experiment to my classmates? An entertainment? Why do they dislike me so much? Because I'm poor? Dirty? Stupid?

I look at Valerie, who's been standing aside, watching me through her glasses like I'm some kind of science project. She's a brainy girl, an A student. Shouldn't she know right from wrong?

I try to walk away nonchalantly, but everyone follows me. A few of my classmates run ahead of me, blocking my way.

"Where do you think you're going, loser?" shouts Joseph, the only boy in the group.

A loser? Me? Didn't he come in second after me in our last school race? I can't believe I used to have a crush on him. I probably just liked his wavy brown hair and curled lip, but his looks seem so shallow now.

Irene, Clara, and Elizabeth, who've been unusually silent so far, launch at me. Grabbing my school satchel out of my hand, they shove me so hard that my feet fly off the ground, and I fall backward into the mud.

I watch in shock as everyone takes something out of my satchel, then hurls it into the surrounding bushes. Even my pens and pencils are swirling in the air like helicopters.

Tears start dripping down my face. How can my classmates be so cruel? I'm crying! I've never understood the enjoyment they get from it. Once I tried to find out what all the fuss with bullying was about, but after I made a girl cry, I cried even more than she did.

"It serves you right," shouts Lucy, kicking my empty satchel at my face.

"Let me be," I plead.

All eight of my classmates come to stand in a circle around me, hovering as I lie on the ground. I cover my eyes with my palms and weep even more. What are they going to do now? Punch me?

I shift my fingers to peek at my classmates, and it makes them laugh harder. I hate them, hate them, hate them! But most of all, I hate myself. I don't deserve anything good. *This* is what I deserve.

"You're disgusting," Lucy speaks again, her face turning serious.

Something breaks inside me, and I push myself off the ground, hitting Lucy on her back with my fist as she tries to get away from me. Then I turn and swing at everyone in my reach. Before I know it, I'm all alone on the path. Only the sound of running steps can be heard in the distance.

It takes some time to find all my things scattered around, buried under the fallen leaves, and coated in mud. The important part of my school uniform—the white satin apron—is ruined. I pull it off, wipe the blood from my scratched palms with it, then hang it on a tree branch. I can't take the apron home for my mother to see it; I don't want to worry her.

As I run home, I try not to think of anything. Not a thing. And when in my kitchen, I put the dump textbooks and notebooks out on the windowsill to dry, then go search for Dad. I've never told him about the bullies, but maybe I should now. At least he might give me some ice cream money to make me feel better.

I open his door and look inside. I don't see him but hear his mumbling voice coming from the balcony. I walk over there and find him lounging in a chair, staring out the window, spaced out. A small glass of vodka is sitting on the floor near his feet. *Oh no.*

Dad doesn't notice me, too busy talking to himself, murmuring. His voice gets lower and lower. He almost starts growling. I know what this means. He's working up his anger toward Mom. I step back and quietly leave him alone.

Surprisingly, Mom is at home too, sitting in her armchair with a cigarette, lost in thought. The smell of the smoke circling in our room seems almost . . . pleasant. It's scary that I'm getting more and more used to it. Mom takes another puff, and I inch away.

"Forgot your bus pass again?" I ask her, hiding my scratched hands from her.

"No. I had a headache, so I returned," she replies, grimacing.

"Citramon to the rescue," I say, quoting a commercial for a headache medicine.

I change my clothes and sit on the edge of my bed, watching Mom take her white yarn and start to knit.

"What are you making?" I ask.

"A hat for a neighbor's order," she replies.

"Hmm . . . extra food money."

I focus on a frying pan sitting on the table beside her. There are fatty onions left floating in the oil.

"Want me to fry potatoes for you?" Mom asks.

"I'm too sleepy for that," I reply. "But I wanna drink cocoa."

"Shh," Mom hisses, putting her forefinger to her pursed lips. "The street cleaner outside could hear you."

"So?"

"He may rob us later."

I roll my eyes. What a ridiculous conclusion. That poor street cleaner is just sweeping the ground. My slogan for life is that most people are naturally good. And no, I don't want to think of my classmates. They'll . . . outgrow their cruelty. *I hope.*

I bury my face in my pillow and decide that I want a nap first. I've been waking up for school so early for five straight days. Why does it have to start at eight? I'm always sleepy, and my mood is . . . ugh.

"If someone ever breaks into our room," Mom says, "grab the knife from the upper drawer and crawl into that corner."

I lift my head apathetically and glance at the spot she's pointing to. My eyes slip to a nearby shelf. There stands a huge black camera.

I bolt upright. "You bought us a camera."

"No, not to us," Mom says and then hurries to explain, "It's a gift for Andrew."

My mouth goes sour. She's secretly in love with her friend's son, who's only eighteen. I understand—he's very, very handsome and has long, curly black hair that flows freely as he rides his motorcycle. But how could Mom be in love with him? She actually told me Andrew was my biological dad. He'd have been what when he fathered me? Eight years old?

And the money . . . I'm sure she spent her meager salary on this. Only she can waste her last rubles on something like this. In May she spent her last cent on a hybrid ring and watch. We'll be eating nothing this month, for sure. And she'll have to knit more than one hat to put bread on our table.

I plop down on my bed and curl up under the blanket, imagining myself as a large turtle hidden under its strong green shell. The darkness forms such a comfortable, safe cocoon, and lulled by my breathing, I easily fall asleep.

I dream of Dad. I see him walking down the hill to the bus stop. I try to run after him, but somehow I'm frozen, paralyzed in the air. As much as I struggle to move, to get to my dad, I can't. He gets farther and farther away, then inevitably, he disappears.

I half wake up from shock, while the other half of me still sees the dream. My eyes move uncontrollably left and right, and I see everything in jigsaw fragments. After my mind clears, I notice the sound of running water coming from our bathroom. The door there is swollen from the humidity and can't be fully closed.

I stay motionless for a minute, then stretch my arms in front of me and get up. Time to make that cocoa and maybe cook something.

Opening the lower cabinet in the kitchen, I pick the three biggest potatoes. I wash them briefly, then peel them with a knife. The dirt makes a mess in the sink. I should have peeled the potatoes while they were dry and only then washed them. I need a container now.

I unlatch the cupboard over my head and take out a deep, wide bowl. Treacherously, it slips from my wet fingers, smashing into hundreds of shards on the floor. *Dang darn dong!*

According to a Russian superstition, if a piece of dishware breaks in your house, great luck is coming your way. It sounds encouraging, but I don't believe in superstitions. The silliest superstition is the one that says that if a black cat crosses your path, bad luck is coming to you. How unfair for the cats! So many people avoid them because of this.

I quickly sweep up the shards, and after throwing them into the trash, I return to the cupboard and take out a new bowl.

"Stole . . . fired . . . fuck . . . will . . ." A few muffled words travel to my ears from a distance.

I tilt my head, straining my ears. Are our neighbors quarreling? That has never happened before. *It's not our neighbors*—it's Dad shouting at Mom.

Goosebumps pop up over my forearms. I drop the bowl on the table and dart to the glass kitchen door. Through it, I see Dad standing in the doorway to the bathroom, holding his rusty axe over his head.

"You stole the calculating machine I was safeguarding for my company," he bellows. "I'm going to kill you for this!"

The lines on Dad's forehead are deep; he's more furious than I've ever seen before. Swinging his axe back and forth over his head, he steps into the bathroom and out of my view.

I hear a splash of water and then Mom's scream. I think I black out for a fraction of a second because the next thing I see is Mom catapulting into the corridor, running across it and toward the front door with water dripping down her naked body.

Dad steps back into the corridor and starts chasing Mom into the entrance hall. What will our neighbors think when they see my mother naked? What a freak show!

"You're a dead woman, Talia!" I hear Dad's voice coming from the porch.

He's not giving up. I stop caring about what the neighbors will think. All I want is for my mother to return home alive. What should I do now?

I lower myself to the floor and crawl into a corner of the kitchen. Clasping my hands in a painful knot, I start to pray. *God, please help my mother escape. Don't let my father catch her. Please, please, please!*

I hear the sound of running outside our kitchen window and dash over to look. There my parents are, running around the building with all their might. Dad is only a yard or so behind Mom, still holding his axe over his head. I shrink against the side wall, feeling like my stomach was kicked, but then the shock gives me energy, and I run to our bedroom, open its door wide, put my hand on the key, and wait for Mom.

It's like I've been looking into a crystal ball. Mom bursts into the apartment right away and runs into the bedroom. I pull the door handle hard and shut the door, turning the key as quickly as I can. Safe, though Mom's bare feet are bleeding slightly now, and she breathes through her mouth like a fish out of water.

"It wasn't you who stole the calculator, was it?" I ask, my own breath coming out in gasps from the shock and relief.

"Of course not," she wheezes out.

What did Dad expect? He forgets to close his door when he's drunk, and there've been some reports of early-morning crooks.

Mom straightens up and goes to her dresser. Opening the upper drawer, she grabs cotton balls, moistens one with some liquid from a bottle, and carefully wipes the cuts on her feet. Next, she opens the lower drawer and pulls out an ampule and syringe. I sigh with frustration. *Not this again.*

Mom often imagines she has one disease or another and buys all kinds of stuff from the local pharmacies that don't ask for prescriptions. *I shouldn't be watching this.*

I go to the window, unlock the safety bars, then jump over the sill to the ground below. The last thing I see as I turn to close the window is Mom twisting her body to pop the syringe needle into her buttock.

The sky is a light purple tonight, like Mom's eyes. Her eyes are actually green, but just now I could've sworn they were violet. Maybe from stress?

As I round the building into the courtyard, I see Olivia and Polina sitting on the bench with their hands resting on the big dance bag they share.

"Hey, girls!" I yell, running toward them. "What's up?"

"We're waiting for our parents," Polina says and smiles at Olivia as she says the same thing with a second-long delay.

How nice would it be to have a sibling, a friend to play with all day long? I'd never get bored, and I'd never be alone when *things* were happening at home.

Mom once told me she'd lost an infant in the past, but I think she was imagining things. When I asked Dad if he'd had other kids in the past, he just shrugged as if he didn't know. How is that possible?

"We're going to dance class," Olivia adds.

"I guessed that," I say, feeling a pang of envious longing. "Do you dance in tutus?"

"No, we do ballet only for a warm-up," Polina replies, looking at me indulgently with her deep brown eyes.

"And then what?"

"Then we practice dances, such as polka, or choreograph dances to songs like 'Where Do Magicians Live?'"

Mr. and Mrs. Kot, Olivia and Polina's parents, appear in the courtyard, and we turn our heads to look at them. Mrs. Kot is wearing fashionable high heels. They're silver and open-toed, showing her bubblegum-pink nail polish. Once again, I wish my mother would wear high heels too, at least sometimes.

Mr. Kot is wearing denim clothes similar to his wife's. Did she choose matching outfits for all of them? Because even Polina and Olivia are wearing jeans today.

The girls wish me goodbye and go to their parents, taking their hands. The four of them start walking up the driveway. All I can see now is a picture of a perfect family. All they're missing is a dog who'd love them to the moon and back.

I get up from the bench and circle the courtyard on my tiptoes, imagining I'm wearing high heels. I also add a stroller with a baby in it. I'm so cool and glamorous, pushing the stroller forward on my super-high heels, and everybody is watching.

I pause and look at the distant figures of Olivia and Polina. What if I secretly follow them to the dance studio? I can watch the girls dance through a window. It would be fun and entertaining. Plus, pretending to be a spy would be fun too.

I walk over to the closest tree in the driveway and stand behind its leafy trunk. Making sure the Kots aren't watching, I dash to the next tree and the next as I follow them down the street. After jumping like a grasshopper for a mile or so, I spot the central Palace of Pioneers and Schoolchildren ahead, which looks more like a tower.

I hide behind a small old plane standing in the middle of the yard for decoration. After the Kots disappear inside the palace, I head for a set of narrow windows on its side and peek inside the first window. It shows the basement settled deep below. Bingo, it's a dance studio!

The hall-like space is beautiful, well-lit, and shiny. Crystal-sharp mirrors surround the room, fronted by wooden ballet barres. Envy squeezes my throat again. What an ugly but familiar feeling. Now that I have a Barbie doll, my next wish is to find tuition money for a dance studio like this.

Maybe I should start saving the pocket money Dad gives me from time to time? I can survive without ice cream, surely. But can I live without the pickled cucumbers I buy from older lady vendors? Hmm . . . I have a goal, and I should try, so by the time I'm a grown-up, I'll have enough money to open my own dance school.

As I watch, two women enter the dance studio, derailing my train of thought. I step aside carefully so they can't see me at the window and watch them surreptitiously. Usually when I stare at someone, they feel my gaze and glance right up at me. This is always spooky. Do we all have some kind of radio transmitter between us? I step even farther away and look down with only one eye, just in case.

One of the women, who has short blond hair, sits down at a shiny black piano and opens the lid, pressing a few keys. The other woman, a tall brunette with a long braid, leans on a ballet bar and talks to the first woman. I assume this second woman is the dance teacher. But where are the students?

My question is answered almost immediately as the main door swings open, and a bunch of kids of different ages pile into the room. Olivia and Polina come last but stand in the front line, facing the mirrors. Where's Ava? She's supposed to be attending dance classes too.

"Turn your feet out," the teacher commands loudly as the first notes of the piano break above the chatter.

I press my forehead to the side of the thin glass pane and try to hear every word she's saying.

"With a soft wave," she continues, floating her wrists down and up gracefully, "move your arms into second position. Now do two *demi-pliés* and one *grand plié.*"

I'm puzzled as to how the kids are able to follow the teacher's every instruction. They know all these foreign words and rarely ask for clarifications. Those who don't understand just look at other kids and repeat after them.

Some of the youngest students are so small and so cute, especially compared to the older students, who are all angles and bones. I can't help but feel jealous of the teacher. Now I want my dance school even more.

"Jump and extend your arms wide," the teacher yells harshly. "And don't forget to *plié* before the jump."

The ballet warm-up ends, and a tape recorder replaces the piano. Now the students start practicing their dance routines to the music of popular songs. "Chunga-Changa" is the merriest of them, and the kids dance in a circle with smiles on their faces.

I stay standing at the window long after the class is over and the lights are turned off. I'm engulfed in my thoughts. Can I teach myself how to dance, since I don't have money for tuition right now? It would be possible, I guess, to use our corridor as a dance room and hum the music to substitute for a player.

I push myself off the wall and run home, taking shortcuts to get there as fast as possible and try out my plan. As the distance becomes shorter, my excitement grows larger. Finally, I pull the front door open and barrel into the corridor.

Doll starts jumping up and down in front of me in her joyful greeting. I put my finger to my mouth for her to be quiet, then listen to the silence in the apartment. I can see darkness under Dad's door. He's asleep, but Mom isn't. Her light is on.

I come closer to our door. "Mom, what are you doing?"

"Knitting," she replies, barely audible. "Should I unlock the door?"

"No, I'll play in the corridor for a while."

With Doll's next jump of excitement, I catch her and say, "You're going to be my dance student today."

I walk to the center of the floor and extend my arms, holding Doll out in front of me. "Let's choreograph a rock-and-roll dance."

I start kicking my legs in the air, recalling as many moves I've seen on TV as I can. Bouncing my knees rhythmically, I repeat over and over, "Pum, pum, pum-pa-rum . . ."

In one swift move, I flip Doll up in the air and send her into a full somersault. Spectacular!

She growls as I catch her, revealing her perfect white teeth.

"I caught you, didn't I?" I ask indignantly.

"Grrrr!"

"I'm your teacher; you should obey me! Let's repeat the dance again. One, two, three . . ."

Chapter Fourteen
A Star

Am I late for school? I raise my head from my pillow and look around. If Mom sees I'm still at home, she'll beat me with my school satchel. *Oh, it's Saturday.* I put my head back down. My mom is at work because she doesn't have official days off, and her salary depends on the collected weight of the tea leaves she gathers each month.

Today and tomorrow, I can do whatever I please and won't have to see my bullies. I'll probably go to Riviera Park, which is about ten minutes from our apartment building. It'll be my "happy as a clam" day. *Riviera.* I roll the Russian *r*. When I was little, I couldn't pronounce it well. The English *r* was so much easier.

Getting up, I tuck my shirt inside my shorts and march into the sunny summer streets buzzing with tourists and activities. In the park, I make sure to smell all the flowers growing along the entrance walkway. The azaleas are crimson and smell of . . . nothing. The pink oleander flowers smell of apricots or peaches. Some long purple flowers smell of dried orange peel and spice. Next time I'll go to the arboretum and smell the thousands of flowers growing there. The locals made a hole in the fence so we could get in free. Bamboo grows in thick walls there, not visible to many.

The fishpond I pass by next should be called a frogpond, lots of frogs and almost no fish. I circle it once and then go into a twisting side alley leading to a sculpture of a goat on a tall pedestal. Impulsively, I climb it, sit on it like on a horse, then watch the tourists below. I bet my neighborhood ladies would love to sit here and gossip.

I see a man and a woman walking, looking like they peed their pants. In actuality, they just pulled their clothes over their wet swimwear, a big no-no in polite society. Following this couple is a group of young Romany women. In contrast to other tourists, they're wearing long skirts. Not one, not two, but at least three, or maybe it's one skirt with multiple layers. And colors . . . the whole rainbow is in there, combining quite beautifully.

Another tourist is walking with a silver camera around his neck. His shirt has palm trees on a blue background, and he's wearing thick socks with flip-flops. I toss my head back and swallow my laugh.

As the man comes closer and takes a picture of the sculpture where I sit, I smile widely for the camera. Other tourists are taking pictures in front of the sculpture too. I don't know what's so special about this goat. Is it even a goat?

Next, a family with kids comes to take a picture, and I realize that the photos with me in them will now travel around Russia, maybe even abroad. As I think that, two Asian men come to the sculpture, give me a thumbs-up, then take turns photographing each other. I wave, and they leave, heading for a metal stand that sells fruit sorbet.

On my left, two older gentlemen are playing checkers. They're dressed in old-fashioned coats that remind me of what the poet Alexander Pushkin is wearing in textbook illustrations.

I carefully climb off the sculpture and drift along the alley with the crowd, looking for something else to pass the time. A vendor is spinning pink cotton candy on a stick to the rhythm of music playing. I immediately feel the sweetness in my mouth from the memory of eating the sugary fluff. It was so irksome that it would dissolve in my mouth before I could even chew it.

I continue moving along the alley past pesky barkers, games, and amusement park rides. Almost all of them are painted red, except for the Ferris wheel towering over the park—its cabins are red, blue, green, and yellow. I need to sneak on for a ride.

I get quietly into the line of ticket holders and hide behind the wide back of a tall woman. I nervously move my hands in and out of my pockets, waiting for her to move. When she and her kids finish showing their tickets to the two collectors, I swiftly shuffle forward with them, leaping up into a moving yellow cabin that's empty.

Smiling like the Cheshire Cat, I slump in my seat and look around to enjoy the expanding view as the cabin rises. I see the river flowing into the sea, creating swirls of different shades of green and blue. Sochi looks like it has more boats, yachts, and catamarans than buildings.

My cabin goes higher and higher in the circle, then suddenly the Ferris wheel lurches, and the cabins start falling backward. I gasp in horror, preparing to die. But before I can work myself into a full panic, the Ferris wheel starts rotating clockwise again. Closer to the ground, I expect to see a team of emergency technicians, but there are only park visitors. Everyone's behaving normally.

I march over to one of the women collecting tickets. Her face is hidden under a white Panama hat with a wide brim.

"What happened to the Ferris wheel?" I ask her.

"What do you mean?" she asks me in return.

I look at her in disbelief. "The wheel was falling backward."

"Oh, we had to roll it back to get a fare dodger out."

The blood rushes from my face. Did someone report me?

An attack is the best defense. "How could you do that? You scared us all to death."

The woman raises her head, and I see her eyes. They look remorseful and apologetic. Now I feel sorry for being so harsh to her.

The day is warm, too warm. I decide to go home. I don't feel well, and I'm thirsty. I cross a river bridge and, on the other side, spot a woman in a ground-floor window in a nearby apartment building. I go closer and ask her for a glass of water.

Maybe the woman has just sprayed herself with perfume, but I smell a strong lavender scent. It instantly evokes a memory of Mom giving me a bubble bath. Isn't it weird that our brains can recall things just like that?

"Sure, just a minute," the woman replies and hurries to the sink.

She hands me a faceted glass through the safety bars, asking, "Are you OK?"

I gulp the water down and nod. After thanking her, I walk across the lawn to the pavement and continue on my way home.

Still, I decide to peek into my courtyard. I can't believe my luck! Kristen, Ava, Victoria, and Anastasia are sitting on the bench.

"Hi, girls," I say, sitting next to them.

"Laura," they squeal.

"I'm happy everyone missed me."

"Of course!" Anastasia says, raising her eyebrows mysteriously. "We need your hyper energy."

I inflate my mouth with air, widen my eyes like saucers, and push my ears out with my fingers. It's all she needs to start laughing, spitting out the pumpkin juice she was drinking. What a waste of deliciously sweet juice, more delicious than apple juice.

"Want me to show you some dance moves I've come up with?" I ask everyone seriously.

"Yes," Kristen replies.

I scoot across the courtyard and up the stairs toward the front yard of the power station and wait for everyone to catch up with me.

"Sit down around the edge," I command.

Anastasia pauses and blows air through a straw into her empty juice box, then she puts the box on the ground and stomps it hard. The loud pop is unexpected, and the scare overwhelms me.

"I'm going to cry," I warn everyone. "Don't pay attention—it's nothing."

I sweep the tears off my cheeks and roll my eyes at myself. The loud sound reminded me of Dad trying to break Mom's and my bedroom door at night.

"Sit, sit," I say to everyone and try to laugh. "The show will start soon."

Anastasia lifts the flattened box off the ground, her forehead furrowed.

"Loud noises scare me too," Ava says sympathetically, chewing on fluffy wisps of her hair.

"I'm ready to dance," I say with a bit of irritation.

I step to the center of the imaginary stage and lift my left foot, then skip to the right and swing my hips left-right-left, then repeat the moves and send myself into a two-rotation turn, raising my arms and bobbing my head. I can improvise on the go.

Unable to sit still, Ava jumps onto our pretend stage and starts dancing too.

"This is how you do it," she says, hopping around the concrete floor, bouncing her elbows up and down, and smiling like she's showing her teeth to a dentist.

Everyone starts clapping for her, and I start clapping too. Maybe her dancing is good, but I don't understand it. The girls attend dance classes—not I—so they know better.

"Let's all dance," Ava offers, and everyone eagerly climbs on the stage.

It's a lot of fun. I don't remember the last time I laughed so much. We dance and whoop and sing Natasha Koroleva songs, copying her eighteen-year-old voice, which sounds almost childlike.

A woman appears at the bottom of the stairs, followed by an older man. We all stop dancing and look at them questioningly.

"Ladies," the woman says and starts walking toward us, "my name is Roxana Ryba. I'd like to invite you to a dance show I'm producing on TV."

Her black velvet dress, dragging a few inches behind her, does look pricey. She may be someone important. The man, on the other hand, is dressed casually and is wearing thick glasses.

"Give us your parents' addresses," he says. "We'll visit them to make an offer."

Kristen is the first to recite her address as we all crowd around the couple, then other girls by turns give their addresses. When my turn comes, I only point to my window at the side of the apartment building and shrug.

The woman scribbles our addresses down in her notepad, then turns to leave.

The man clears his throat, then asks, "What time would it be the best to catch your parents at home?"

"One of my parents is usually always at home," I answer first.

The couple gives each other a look, seeming to be disappointed. Am I imagining things?

When they leave, we stay standing in a cluster, discussing the possibilities.

"Why do you want to be stars?" Ava asks us.

"For me, it's traveling the world," I reply.

"Giving autographs," Kristen says uncertainly.

Victoria giggles. "Our teachers will give us As just because we're famous."

"I'd like to have enough money to buy all the shoes I want," Anastasia says.

"Yes, all that." Kristen nods. "And my dad will visit me more often."

We turn to look at her with compassion. Except Ava. She is staring at her hands. Her dad is dead. No amount of stardom would ever bring him back.

"I need to run home and tell my parents," I say. "And so do you."

"Yes, let's go," Anastasia says.

I zoom past our neighbors sitting on the bench and run to my apartment.

"Dad!" I yell, pulling the front door open.

"What?" he asks.

Thank goodness, his voice is sober. I take a few steps toward his room, then stop to check if Mom is home. She's not, so I continue into Dad's room. I find him in the adjacent room, which is our spare room. If I didn't like being always close to Mom, I'd have made this my room.

"The girls and I were offered a spot as dancers on TV," I say triumphantly.

"By whom?" Dad asks and sticks his tongue out. It means he's concentrating deeply. I look at what he's doing. He's repairing the wooden window frame that connects this room to our glass balcony.

I sigh, feeling put down by Dad's lack of interest but try to keep my enthusiasm up. "A woman and a man saw us dancing and thought we could be stars in their show."

"Adults shouldn't talk to kids without their parents present," Dad says. "Stranger danger, remember?"

"They took our addresses—to talk to you."

"What? You gave them your addresses?" Work forgotten, Dad turns to look at me in shock.

I feel confused by his reaction. "Yes. And we gave them the times when our parents are at home."

Dad shakes his head and says, "They could be criminals who want to know the times we're *not* home. Who else gave their addresses?"

"Victoria, Ava, Kristen, and Anastasia."

"I'll talk to their parents."

Wow, Dad is taking this seriously, not in the way I hoped. I trail back into the corridor. Now that I think of it, the couple did look somewhat sketchy. I can't pinpoint what it was, but something was wrong. Well, my dreams of becoming a dancer are dashed again. *Sweet tea to the rescue.*

Our dogs are lying in the kitchen under the window, basking in the sun's rays. I put the kettle on the stove and squat to stroke Doll's head.

"Forgive me for yesterday's somersaults," I say.

I kiss her muzzle, and she licks my face in return. It's wonderful—dogs never hold a grudge for long.

After drinking tea, I go to Mom's and my bedroom, grab my brown tights, and pull them on my head as a wig. The legs feel just like two long braids hanging over my shoulders.

I run into the corridor and strike an opening pose for a lambada dance. Singing a garbled imitation of the lyrics to a Portuguese song, I start moving to the rhythm, bouncing my hips from side to side and lifting my legs.

As I stamp loudly around the floor, an idea strikes me. I partly open Mom's and my bedroom door and jump onto it. This is going to be my dance partner tonight. I start swaying and swinging, making the door rock and swing in a half circle.

Holding on for so long isn't easy, but I manage. For the next loop of the repeating melody, I slide onto the floor into a split and bend back.

Suddenly, the front door opens, and Mrs. Zayka appears in the crack.

"Why is it so loud in here?" she asks.

"Ah!" I yelp, frightened by the unexpected interruption.

"Laura, the noise is giving me a headache."

I jump to my feet and tug the embarrassing wig off.

"Oh," Mrs. Zayka says. "You've been dancing."

That's right, *oh*. I'm so irritated. I was dancing and having so much fun. Why did she have to break the spell?

"I'll be quiet," I say. *Because I won't be dancing anymore.*

"Wait," she says. "I'll call for Angelina and Natalie. I'm sure they'd like to see you dance."

My eyebrows shoot up. "What about your headache?"

"Just land with the tips of your toes and your knees bent, and you'll be quiet."

"How do you know that?"

"I took some folk dance classes when I was young."

"Really?"

Mrs. Zayka has already disappeared from my doorway. A minute later, she reappears with her twin granddaughters. I'm going to have an audience of two seventeen-year-olds and an older lady. Is my lambada even ready for that?

The girls smile at me in an unspoken promise of no harsh judgment, and my worries fade. I start to dance.

"Sway your hips more," Natalie urges.

"Show how," I say.

She laughs, removes a hair tie from her damp hair, and starts dancing.

"Draw a number eight with your hips," Angelina says, bossing us around.

"Dance with us too," I tell her.

She arches her legs, playing with her short, flowing skirt and laughing. I try to repeat the movements after the twins as much as I can and look at Mrs. Zayka for reassurance each time.

The headache seemingly out of mind, she's tapping her foot joyfully while my dogs sit at her feet.

"One, two, three; one, two, three," Natalie chirps like a singsong bird.

"Did a bear step on your ear?" Angelina asks her. "It's one, two, three, four, five. Uh-huh, yes, just like that."

Angelina turns, lifts me up, and sways me around the floor, just like I swayed Doll yesterday. I squeal with glee. What a wonderful day! It's like Christmas and New Year's Eve rolled into one.

Chapter Fifteen
Forgetting to Say Goodbye

The next morning I wake up and start thinking of new ideas for how to make money. I think and think and think, and the best idea that has come so far is to sell some of the tea leaves Mom baked yesterday. I can go to an open-air market near the seaport and do it there. I only have to find something I can use as a package.

Mom keeps the tea leaves in a fishbowl. I can take some of it easily without Mom noticing. I get out of bed and walk around the apartment, examining every item in sight. In the bathroom, I see three colorful soap cases and instantly know they'll serve as boxes perfectly.

I wash and dry them thoroughly, then scoop the tea and fill the boxes to the brim. Next, I glue paper on top of the cases and write different prices. Although they're all the same size, I know that some people like to buy the most expensive things, while others the cheapest, and still others like to buy what's in the golden middle.

I drop the cases into a shopping bag and hurry out the front door. I'm surprised and ticked off to discover that it's started raining. There won't be many customers out in the street in such weather. It would be smart to give up, but I don't like giving up.

Drops of rain drum on my face and fall on the pavement in big crystals. I raise the bag over my head and run up the driveway and down the street. Ugh, I hate being wet.

"Girl," a man shouts from a car parked nearby. "Am I heading in the right direction for the Sputnik movie theater?"

He's chewing on the earpiece of his sunglasses as I come closer so he'll hear my explanation.

"This is the wrong direction," I say, trying not to gawk at his eye, which looks like a rusty nail was forgotten there. "You should—"

At this moment, the man moves aside the newspaper he's been holding, revealing a long *thing* sticking out from his unbuttoned pants. *Another pervert.*

I jump a few feet back and try not to vomit, then dart to the underpass that takes me to Sycamore Alley, where dozens of white iron stalls line the pathway to the sea esplanade.

On a sunny day, hundreds of tourists roam this area but not today. No customers and no competition either—all the stalls are empty. I choose the one that faces the administration building where brides and grooms come to say their "I do's." Maybe some weddings will take place this morning.

I get behind the counter and sweep away the drops of water, then carefully lay my tea boxes out. I open one to display the oven-dried black leaves and plaster a smile on my face. *Come, buyers, come.*

No one's paying attention to me. A few people who do pass by are hidden under their huge umbrellas. Today our city seems deserted. Where are all those millions of tourists we're supposed to have each summer?

I wish I'd stayed at home and drunk hot tea. Half an hour goes by, forty minutes, fifty... Only one man stopped to examine my tea boxes. He eyed the tea, then me, then the tea again, and curling his long mustache between his fingers, he gave me one more puzzled look and left without buying anything.

The shopping aisles start to flood, and I'm getting chilly. Alas, I need to go. I sweep the tea boxes back into the bag and scurry away.

The rain eases as I near my apartment building, and the wet street starts reflecting the light skidding from the clouds. What a beautiful day it's becoming. I stop to smell the jasmine bush beckoning me with its aroma. There's another hint of smell in the air. I look around and find a bush of tiny roses growing in clusters. Only after the rain can the flowers smell so awesome. The combination reminds me of the girly perfume I've smelled on Polina and Olivia.

Something rustling in the pine tree on my left makes me take a step back and look up—there's a brown squirrel. Sensing my gaze, it comes to a stop and stares back at me with eager black eyes.

"I'll bring you sunflower seeds later," I promise, and as it jumps on another branch and runs up the trunk, I continue on my way too.

Ava is walking in the courtyard, hidden under her cute yellow umbrella with bumblebees printed on it. As she sees me, she starts running in circles, shouting hoorays.

"You seem happy to see me," I say, secretly pleased.

"Yes!" she yells. "Let's jump in the puddles together."

I look at my lacy white dress. Although I slept in it, it was still clean in the morning. Not now though. It's drenched and clinging to my body. I may as well jump in those dirty puddles.

"Alright then," I say and toss the bag of tea onto the bench.

Ava grabs my hand and moves us to the first puddle. Squatting like a frog, she hops up and jumps into it. *Splash!*

"Jump with me," she admonishes.

"Easy for you to say," I retort. "You're in rubber boots."

She squeezes my wrist and, giggling, leads us to another puddle.

"What's the sense of you holding your umbrella up if you spatter us with rainwater each time?" I ask.

"Not to get my hair wet," she replies. "It's difficult to comb it."

"You sound like you have a lisp. Have you lost a baby tooth or something?"

"Uh-huh. A mouse stole it."

"A mouse?"

"Yes."

I smirk and look up at the sky. The clouds have parted and unveiled the sun with its bright, beautiful halo.

"I better go home," Ava says, also looking at the sky and closing her umbrella.

"Why?" I ask. "The rain puddles are still here."

"I locked George in the bathroom."

"You did what? You're kidding me!"

"No, I was mischievous."

"But why did you do that?"

"I got a call from the man who offered us the TV job yesterday, but George grabbed the phone away from me and was rude to him," she says.

I instantly perk up. "The man? I thought the woman was the producer, not the man."

"No, he said he was a producer too."

"How did he get your phone number?"

She shrugs. "Maybe he called zero nine, where they give the phone information."

"And let me guess. He called not at the time you said your parents were at home?"

"No. Didn't they call you too?"

"I don't have a telephone, remember?" I say. "George was right to be rude, so go unlock the door."

I wish her a good day and head home to finally warm myself up with tea and a blanket. As I step over the threshold, I realize that Mom is home. I hear her in our room, moving around. I freeze in my tracks. Thank goodness I forgot the bag of tea in the courtyard. I unfreeze myself and walk into the room.

"Didn't you go to work?" I ask nonchalantly.

"I went to the plantation but not to work," she replies.

She's wearing stilettos. I'm surprised. Just the other day, I wished she'd put on high heels, and here she is, in them. This surprise, however, is quashed by another surprise. There, on my mother's bed, lies an open, half-filled suitcase.

"Where are you going?" I ask, my breath rushing out of me in a gasp.

"You and I, we both are going," she replies.

"But where?"

"To the tea plantation. What's wrong with your dress? Change it and dry your hair with a towel."

"OK, and will you pack my clothes too?"

She bows her head. "Of course."

"How long will we be there?" I ask.

"Forever. We don't want to stay here with that bastard."

"Oh . . . I see. And where are we staying?"

"At my friend's house. Eve is a decent woman of faith, and she has a daughter your age. It'll be lots of fun for you."

Of faith? Mom has never talked about God. I'm the only kid in our neighborhood who hasn't been baptized. *Whatever.*

I go to my wardrobe and change into my flowery green romper slowly and unexcitedly, realizing that I don't want to move out of our apartment. But . . . I won't have to go back to the same school and deal with my bullies again. That's very good.

I tousle my hair like models do in shampoo commercials and leave it sticking up. Then I go stand by the window and watch Mom finish packing.

As she takes her passport out of the drawer and zips the suitcase, Dad's door cracks open, and he shuffles out, looking sick and disheveled. He probably drank yesterday before bed.

He glances into our room, and his eyes zero in on the suitcase immediately. Long minutes go by, then his shoulders slump forward.

"Uh," he croaks, stepping into our room. "Are you leaving?"

Mom's face hardens. She doesn't answer, and Dad's eyes fill with tears. He turns around and looks at me, smoothing back his greasy silver hair. Right now he seems like the saddest dad on earth. My heart aches for him, and I want to weep. *I'm sorry, Daddy, I'm sorry.*

Mom stuffs her yarn into her handbag, closes the wardrobe doors, then lifts the suitcase and walks out into the corridor, past Dad.

I follow her, turning around to look for the dogs but not seeing them anywhere. Pity I won't be able to say goodbye to them. On the other hand, I don't have to. I can visit them as often as I want.

Mom and I arrive at the tea plantation in less than an hour, making good time. The suitcase isn't heavy, so I take it from Mom's hand and let her focus on walking carefully up the mountain in her stilettos. I bet she regrets wearing them now. Their clicking and echoing ricochets against the concrete road's surface, drawing everyone's attention.

The leaves on the bushes and trees reflect the sunlight, glittering like gold. It doesn't look like it rained here today. Beads of sweat drip down our foreheads—it's that hot.

"Strange that the snake isn't here today," Mom mumbles.

"What snake?" I ask curiously.

"The one that follows me to work in the mornings."

"That's horrible. Yuck!"

"No, it is friendly and talks to me."

Talks to her? I'd better not argue, or it'll upset her, as always. I just hope I won't lose my mind one day, like she did.

I distract myself by staring at the animals roaming about. Horses are wandering along the sides of the road like stray cats. And I see a bull in the distance. I cringe in fear. Mom and I aren't wearing anything red, thank goodness. But . . . why is it staring at me like that?

I shift my eyes away, pretending not to be scared. A few dozen yards ahead of us, a short man with a half-bald, wrinkled head is standing at the side of the road, staring at my mother. *Another starer?*

"Who's that man?" I ask Mom, nudging her with my elbow.

She looks up and immediately grabs my arm. "Let's pass him fast."

Is she overreacting again?

"Taalia," the man calls to her pleadingly, stretching her name as if it has four syllables. "Please stop and talk to me!"

Maybe not overreacting. The man is weird.

"Leave me alone!" Mom tells him and grabs the suitcase from my hand so I can run faster.

"So who's that man?" I ask Mom again after we pass him.

"A stalker," she replies.

"Huh? Just tell him you're married."

"I did."

The man continues calling out. "Talia! Give me a minute. Can I catch up?"

Mom turns and growls at him, "No."

The mountain road takes us farther away from the man, and I relax my grip on Mom's hand. "Does he bother you like that often?"

"Every day," she answers, shaking her head irritably. "Wherever I'm working in the field, he finds me."

"That's not good."

"Do you think I'd better kill him?"

"Noooo!" I yelp. "Of course not. I told you—the police always solve the crimes."

"I can feed his body to some pigs. No one will ever know."

"You won't get away with it," I say calmly, but I'm not calm. Deep inside, I have the urge to yell at her so my breath would hit her like a storm.

Her words still hang in the air as we continue walking, sending shock waves through me. That was a new low for her, the most horrible thing she'd ever said. This. Is. Sick.

"Just ask your friends to help you with him," I say tiredly.

"They won't help me," she responds in a detached voice. "They refused to help me with killing my husband."

"That's not what I meant!"

Bile fills my mouth. *How could she?* I shouldn't talk to her anymore. I wish I were somewhere else where I could cry. When was the last time I allowed myself to just cry freely? To cry with frustration, with despair, with the hopelessness of it all.

With a guilty conscience, I brood over the unfairness of having this mother out of all the mothers in the world. Yet again, I'm envious of my friends and wondering how it would feel to have a normal mother. Why do *I* always have to be the different one?

"Smile," Mom tells me as we enter a small driveway to a single-story wooden house.

I look up, and right on cue, the front door opens, and a woman as thin as a birch steps out onto the wide porch, followed by a lanky red-haired girl.

"Meet Mrs. Volk and her wonderful daughter, Jane," Mom says to me loudly.

I look at Jane shyly, noticing that she's studying me too. She has on a blue dress with dangling threads, black leggings, and dirty white shoes. Although she's smaller than me, she's supposed to be my age. Will we be friends, or even like sisters?

"You're welcome to our house," Mrs. Volk says, her deep-set eyes twinkling at the corners.

She puts a warm hand on my arm, then draws me into a hug. "It's a very simple house that we have, but I hope you'll like it."

"I've never lived in a house," I tell her earnestly. "I'll love it."

Mrs. Volk laughs heartily and winks at Mom conspiratorially. "Kids can be so charming."

I peek at Jane again. Although her hair looks ginger red, and mine is sandy, we could be easily mistaken for sisters. My dream of having a sibling is finally coming true.

She isn't shy at all. Grabbing me by the hand, she leads me into the house and straight to her room—*now my room too*. It's clean and spacious, with so many possibilities to play. I go to the window and look at the view. It's . . . well, rustic. And spectacular. Horses, cows, and lambs are grazing in the meadow, which is dotted with small yellow, blue, and purple flowers.

I sneeze, and Jane laughs.

"Don't look at the sun like that," she says. "And by the way, this is your bed under the window."

I take a few steps back and look at the bed in awe. It has two pillows lying on each other. They're so big that I'll be able to look at the meadow while lying down. Maybe I'll even be able to see the planets at night.

The linens on the bed look crisp, inviting. I can smell the scent of laundry detergent. Mountain breeze or something. I'm going to stay in bed all day tomorrow and read my English textbook. It'll be so cozy.

"Do you have any friends around here?" I ask, turning to Jane.

"Yes, Nora and Zara," she answers.

"What about boys?"

She scrunches up her small, freckled nose. "Meh, I don't think of them at all."

I chuckle. "They can actually be fun to hang out with."

I look further around the room. There's a round rug on the floor I can dance on if I move the chairs away from it. The other prominent thing in the room is a TV set on a short trestle table. Its images are flashing silently, but as Jane notices my interest, she walks over to it and turns the sound up.

A slim man with long black hair is dancing and singing on the screen. Goosebumps start popping on my arms. He's out of this world.

"Michael Jackson." Mom's mellow voice comes from behind me.

I turn to look at her. She's bouncing her feet in time to the music while holding a tray of freshly baked rolls. It's only when the music video gives way to commercials that she steps out of the doorway and goes back to the kitchen. Wow, I never knew she was a fan of . . . Michael Jackson.

I go to the window again and look outside. Now two tiger-colored cats have joined the cows and are cavorting between their legs. I reconcile myself to the idea of living here. It's going to be pretty tolerable.

Chapter Sixteen
Daddy Is Asleep

We've been living at the tea plantation for over a week now. As my mother predicted, it's been nothing but fun. Roosters wake us with their high-pitched crowing every morning before dawn, and we start our adventures early. Mrs. Volk gives us fresh goat's milk to drink for breakfast, and afterward, Jane and I go play outside. Sometimes I go help my mother pick tea leaves instead.

I've come to appreciate how difficult and monotonous her job is. She's settled into routine well and doesn't miss a day at work. Every ruble she earns is well-deserved.

Jane snaps her fingers in front of my face. "Get your head out of the clouds and help me with the buckets, will ya?"

"Yes," I reply grumpily.

She's drawing water from the well in the backyard. Taking one full bucket from her, I follow her into the house.

"Your hair is very red in the sun," I notice as we climb the stairs.

She giggles, covering her mouth with her bony fingers. "Mom wanted to throw me from the hospital window when I came out a redhead."

"No way!"

She doesn't laugh, and my eyes bug out. Is she really serious?

"My mom likes redheads," I say. "She even made rag dolls, painting their hair with her red lipstick."

"That's nice," Jane says, smiling. "My mom likes my red hair now too."

A yellow butterfly brushes against her nose, making her almost drop her bucket of water.

"Aren't you special?" I tease. "Even butterflies think you're a flower."

"What?" she asks, and then it dawns on her. "Yes, I'm a calendula."

Laughing, we cross the boardwalk wrapping around the house and step through the back door right into the kitchen.

"Now feed the chickens in the henhouse," Mrs. Volk says after we leave the buckets by the table. "And then you're free to play."

Being the obedient child she is, Jane agrees immediately and dutifully rushes back outside.

I pause and turn to Mrs. Volk. "Do you know where my mother is? I went to the tea fields today, and she wasn't there."

"I don't know, sweetheart," Mrs. Volk replies after thinking for a second. "She left very early, wearing a dress. Could that mean she went to downtown Sochi?"

I nod. That explains a lot.

"Laura," Mrs. Volk calls after me as I turn to leave. "I like having you live with us. Jane has become much more active, running around with you all day."

I smile to myself. Usually the parents of my friends don't like me for this very reason. It feels nice that Mrs. Volk appreciates this.

"And I like having your mother around," Mrs. Volk adds. "She's smart, generous, and very grateful."

I look up at the ceiling, giving myself time to think. Mom is generous and grateful, but . . . how do her friends manage not to notice that she's *different*? Do they believe her fantasy-ridden stories? Well, Mom called Mrs. Volk a woman of faith. Maybe that's what makes a person loving and accepting.

I exit the house, trying to remember how many friends Mom actually has. Not many. Most of them just stopped visiting us at some point or another in the past. But she has Mrs. Volk now. I'm glad.

"Why do you look so sad?" Jane asks, meeting me halfway down the path to the henhouse. She's already fed the chickens and is returning.

Am I sad? I wasn't this morning. Now, though, I feel some sense of dread and foreboding. I wanna go to bed and lie down.

Jane is still waiting for an answer. I make a sweeping gesture around us and say, "I sometimes think that everything I like will disappear eventually."

"Don't be ridiculous. Snap out of it. Let's play."

Easy for you to say.

"Tag!" Jane yells and runs to the meadow, away from me. "You're It."

I shake off my awful feeling and run after her. "Not for long."

We play tag for half an hour before switching to hopscotch. Jane takes chalk from a box hidden under the porch and draws a diagram of squares and numbers on the asphalt. I'm confused about the rules of this game, so I just hop randomly, losing each time.

"Have you ever jumped elastics?" I ask.

"No," Jane answers.

"I'll teach you."

I walk over to one of the windows and call for Mrs. Volk. When she appears, I ask her to give me three yards of the elastic she was using for sewing belts yesterday, and then, with it in hand, I return to Jane.

"Interesting," she comments as I tie the elastic into a circle, then loop it around a tree stump.

"Step into the loop and walk back to stretch the elastic," I say to her.

"What now?" she asks, bewildered.

"Watch," I say and start jumping over the elastic lines in different combinations.

"Now I want to do it," Jane squeals.

I stand in her place and watch in astonishment as she starts hopping even better than me, improving with each new round, going from the level where the elastic is around my ankles to where the elastic is around my knees.

Tired afterward, we go to a cypress tree, perch on adjoining branches, and just talk. Later Mrs. Volk calls for us to come for dinner.

We eat and also watch TV for a few hours, then Jane pulls me along outside, carrying the bologna sandwiches her mom made for us.

Jane and I walk around the front yard to the rhythm of our chewing. The sandwiches even have butter in them. Yummy. Everything Mrs. Volk cooks is yummy.

"Your mother is great," I tell Jane with a sigh.

"And yours isn't?" Jane asks.

I frown at her. "Why would you ask that?"

"I heard your mom used to forget to pick you up from the day care center and kindergarten you attended here at the tea plantation."

"It was the buses that didn't come on time, not my mother."

"Hmm."

"Will Zara and Nora come out to play with us?" I ask, changing the subject.

My question doesn't register with Jane. She's staring into the distance.

"Why does your mother always wear heavy makeup?" she asks.

I turn to look in the direction of her gaze. At the far end of the driveway, my mother's silhouette is slowly heading toward the light of our yard. As she gets closer, I focus on her makeup. The blue eyeliner is garish, clashing with her green eyes. The thick layer of red lipstick makes her already very plump lips look clownish. But why does her skin look so pale?

I turn to Jane and ask her harshly, "What's wrong with wearing makeup?"

"It's bad for your health," she replies, sounding judgmental.

Instantly, my mind starts painting pictures of Mom's makeup going through her skin, into her bloodstream, harming her. I've played with Mom's makeup myself and put it all over my face, scaring Dad. Did he think I damaged my health?

I look back at Mom but can't focus on her makeup anymore. She has a deer-in-the-headlights expression; her eyes are wide, not blinking at all.

I start walking toward her. "Mom?"

"Say goodbye to Jane," she says quietly. "We're returning home."

"But . . ."

"Now."

"I need to retrieve—"

"Tomorrow."

Tomorrow.

"Let's go, Laura," she says in an even quieter voice.

I turn to Jane, say an apologetic goodbye to her, and promise to come back tomorrow. Then I follow Mom down the mountain and toward the bus stop.

She's wearing a white-and-navy blue dress today. I frown. I could've sworn she didn't bring it to the tea plantation, but I may be wrong. Mom says the only thing I remember well is song lyrics.

I stumble, realizing that my days of not going to school are over now. My school uniform and satchel are waiting for me at home.

"Do I have to go to school tomorrow?" I ask reluctantly.

"Yes," Mom replies absentmindedly.

"Can't I beg off?"

"No."

Mom confuses two shortcuts, so distracted. I have to call for her a few times to make her turn back and change direction.

At the bus stop, instead of sitting on its bench, she walks to the stairs leading to the village's theater called Culture House and sits on the upper step there.

I sit down next to her and watch her pull out a pack of cigarettes and light one up. When she finishes it, she lights up another. Over the next hour, she continues to chain-smoke while staring out into the nothingness, like she's forgotten I'm even there.

I lay my head on my knees and try to remember all the fun Jane and I usually had in the evenings. Does she already miss me? No, she'll have Nora and Zara to entertain her tomorrow. Plus, she likes going to school, and her classmates are good, totally different from mine.

It's pitch dark by the time bus number 120 arrives. We run to it, and our little endeavor makes Mom cough violently.

"You should quit smoking," I tell her as we board the bus.

"No, my lungs are already destroyed," she says and takes a seat by the window.

"Go to a doctor."

"I'll just drink some hair conditioner. It'll help."

I bite my lip to keep from saying anything and go take a seat at the back of the bus. Despite the roar of the engine, I feel sleepy, and the rocking seems tranquil. I lean against the side and give in to the wonderful sensation.

"Wake up." I hear Mom's voice from a distance. "Time to change buses."

I straighten up and try to stand, but my legs feel half-numb, half-pins-and-needles. In a big effort, I push myself up with the help of the handrails and exit the bus on bent knees.

Brr . . . it's cool outside. My teeth start to chatter. Weird, it's only September twenty-first. Or is it twenty-second? Twenty-third? When I don't go to school, I lose track of the date.

Goosebumps break out over my arms. From the cold? From the apprehension? I have such a terrible feeling. What can it be? *Bed . . . I need my bed.* I'm just tired.

Our next bus comes quickly. We hop on it and take the seats closest to the front. Mom is totally oblivious to the bus driver, who keeps glancing at her and trying to catch her eye.

The five stops before ours fly by, and we stand up, preparing to exit at the Moscow Hotel stop.

"Ladies," the driver says playfully, "I'm going to drive you right to your house. Where do you live?"

Mom looks at him blankly and doesn't answer, so I answer for her. "Turn to the right after reaching the courthouse."

The passengers gasp as the driver does just that, turning his long, bulky bus onto the hill and driving straight to our apartment building.

"Thank you very much," I say to him after the bus lurches to a stop at the foot of our street stairs.

Mom still shows no reaction. We get off the bus, and the driver waves at me with his large hand. I wonder briefly if his hands grew this large because he's been turning the wheel of the bus for so long. Probably not.

The remnants of my sleepiness disappear by the time we get to our apartment. Dad will be so excited to see me. I go to his door and knock.

"Dad!" I yell. "I'm home."

I wait patiently for a minute for him to come and open the door, but he doesn't.

I knock again, more loudly this time. "Dad, wake up!"

No answer. I start pounding the door with my fists. "Daaad!"

Nothing.

"Dad?" I press my ear to the door and listen. Silence.

"Dad! Open! The! Door!" I shout, punctuating every word with a kick.

How can he be sleeping so soundly? He's probably drunk. I bend down and look through the keyhole. Darkness. I grab the handle and rattle it. Nada. I give up.

Mom has been watching me impassively through our open bedroom door, smoking another cigarette. I walk in and sit on the floor, deciding to play for a while before bed. I've missed my Barbie so much. I didn't want to take her to the plantation, because I didn't want others to play with her.

I imagine she's having her wedding day. I don't have a Ken doll for her, but I use a blue marker instead, envisioning it as Ken. I myself will be a guest at their wedding. I need to buy a gift for them.

I reach for my mother's purse and fish out her wallet. I'll be both the customer and the salesperson at the gift store. Opening Mom's wallet, I slip out the only bill it has—5,000 rubles. Wow, I didn't know Mom had so much money. Maybe I can ask her to buy me a toy piano? I've wanted to learn to play for so long.

I fold and unfold the bill, listening to its relaxing, crispy sound and touching the paper's uneven texture. Something about the purple-red banknote keeps bothering me. I examine it more closely. On its white edge are pencil-scribbled doodles. *My doodles.*

"Why do you have Dad's money?" I ask, my eyes narrowing.

Mom hesitates before answering. "It's my money."

"No, it's not."

I lift the bill up to the light and wait for her to look down at it. "See the doodles? I drew them on Dad's money when he got his pay on September sixth."

"He gave it to me," she says dismissively.

I sincerely doubt that. She probably stole it. I'm at a loss for words, but what can I say to her?

I tuck the bill back into her wallet and walk over to my bed. I'll finish playing tomorrow.

Crawling under the blanket, I relax into my soft pillow and close my eyes. I don't mind falling asleep with the lights on. It feels like I'm sleeping in the comfort of the cheery sun. Mom often knits throughout the night, though she isn't knitting now. The cigarette smoke has filled the room, creating a haze. At this rate, Mom will have to spend the 5,000 rubles on new packs of cigarettes. I remember I once gathered fifty cigarette butts from the streets so Mom could save money on her habit, but she didn't appreciate the gesture and forbade me to do it again.

There's a lull in Mom's smoking. She's busy staring at her arms.

"What's wrong?" I ask.

"I have shingles on my skin," she replies.

"Nuh-uh."

She jumps to her feet. "I'll use salicylic acid on it. It'll burn the virus."

I wince. The last time she used acid to burn her imaginary illnesses, her face got so swollen, I couldn't see her eyes in the deep, sticking folds of the red flesh.

As she goes into the corridor, I turn onto my side and study the patterns in the wallpaper. Flowers in yellow. I trace them with my finger and try to fall asleep. But it's only when my mother returns—seemingly unharmed—that I'm able to do so.

Chapter Seventeen
Mother or Father

The alarm clock goes off too soon for my liking. I reluctantly get up and go to the open window. I desperately need a breath of fresh air. Mom is still sitting on her bed, smoking. Ugh! Has she even gone to bed? The lights are all on.

Breathing in the moist morning air, I turn and offer Mom a smile. Her eyes are glazed and vacant. She seems to have aged overnight. Some distant thought is holding her in place, or maybe she's just tired from lack of sleep. I sigh and go to the kitchen sink to brush my teeth. After that, I make myself tea and return to the room to get dressed.

As I brush my hair, I look at Mom again. She's watching me now with wide-open eyes, finally paying attention. I smile at her one more time, then grab my school satchel and head for the corridor.

Before I exit the room, I turn and look at Mom yet again.

"Goodbye, Sasha-Love," she says.

Sasha? Will I forever be Sasha to her? It sounded so warm that I don't mind if she calls me that forever.

"Goodbye, Mommy," I say and walk out into the corridor.

I amble toward the school mindlessly, looking at the blue sky above, which seems to go on forever. At the stairs to the school's main entrance, a woman, probably a teacher going to work, stops and tells me to look back.

I turn and see that there's Doll. Oh, she's been trailing after me since I left home. How haven't I noticed her? What a sneaky little girl!

"You can't come to school," I say, squatting in front of her. "Go back home."

In amazement, I watch her do just that. What a clever dog! A few kids try to stop her and stroke her fur.

"Good dog," a boy tells her, smiling with his braces on full show.

"Yours?" a girl asks me.

"Yes," I answer and then add a lie, "Her mother was a famous circus performer."

"Really?"

"Really."

"Are you going to class now?"

"Yep."

"Let's walk together. My name is Anna."

Wow, Doll is making me popular. Even a cool girl like Anna, with her expensive-looking golden chain and bracelet, doesn't mind talking to me now.

"Anna, nice to meet you," I say eagerly. "My name is Laura." *Or Sasha.* A flash of memory of Mom's warm voice fills my chest with a fuzzy feeling.

The school day starts, and I begin my work, listening to the lectures, watching demonstrations, and taking notes. None of the knowledge goes into my head, though. Thoughts of the tea plantation are whirling in my mind. I'm going to go there today, have dinner with Jane, play with her, then retrieve my things and return home. Planning, planning, planning. I'll go home to drop off my satchel and change my clothes once school lets out. If Dad has snacks, I'll hang out with him and then begin my trip.

Finally, classes are over! Sweeping my textbooks from the desk, I hurry out of the classroom. The bullies won't catch up with me. The first minutes after the school-bell are the most critical for getting far ahead of them.

My pace is fast; I imagine myself being an arrow as I run. It helps, and I keep this pace right until I reach Voykova Street. None of my classmates live here. I'm safe. No one has ever bullied me in my neighborhood. George did a little in the past, but he kept it mainly humorous. There was also a weird teenager who liked to come to our courtyard to show his bare bottom, but I ignored him mostly.

As my tension melts away and I relax, I start thinking of the things Jane and I can do together today. Choreograph dances with umbrellas? Or hats? Or ribbons? Yes, ribbons, but the special kind that's used for bows and is very long and light. But where will we get them?

Lost in thought, I round the corner of the apartment building, walk along the pathway, climb the five steps to the porch, and turn into my entrance hall. I see a uniformed policeman standing at our wide-open front door, staring inside intently.

The strangeness of it doesn't register, and I continue walking, just mildly curious about why he's there. When he notices me, he immediately turns to walk toward me. In a few strides, he comes over and blocks my way.

Taking off his blue-and-red cap, he says, "You can't go in there."

All the blood drains from my face, and a wave of terror engulfs me, shaking me to the bone, bringing a horrible image into my mind: Mom lying on Dad's couch with a knife sticking out of her naked body, limp, stabbed to death.

"Mother or Father?" I ask calmly.

Averting his dark eyes, the officer reluctantly answers, "Father."

Father, father, father. I stare at the officer without seeing him, waiting for his voice to stop reverberating in my head. The floor beneath my feet sways, and my head flops down as if filled with stones. I make an effort to move, slowly turn away, and go downstairs to the courtyard.

In a daze, I drop my satchel in the bushes behind the bench and sit down. Staring ahead blindly, I think of how unreal it seems that a person, such an important person, can be alive one day and then not alive the next. Can just one moment, one second, cause such a difference? How can this world go on without my dad, who was an essential part of its being?

Is he completely gone from existence? Or does his soul still live, watching me? The breath I've been holding tingles in my throat, and I open my mouth to let it out, then suck in the air. Why haven't I noticed before there's not enough of it?

Did Mom kill Dad today or . . . or . . . He wasn't asleep yesterday, was he? Why are bad things happening to me? Why would the universe even bother? I'm not interesting. I'm not important.

A tawny stray cat comes down the driveway and curls up at my feet. It doesn't seem real either. It probably doesn't exist.

"Laura," a neighbor with artfully shaggy hair calls from her window. "Do you want to come up and eat?"

She knows. How? It means everyone knows. I shake my head. It wouldn't be respectful toward my dad to eat now. Besides, I wouldn't have been able to swallow anything anyway.

I suddenly realize that a lot of neighbors must be watching me from their windows now, judging me. Do they expect me to cry? Should I? I don't want to. I just feel . . . numb.

A jarring, clattering noise makes me turn and look with confusion at the empty corner of the building. Then two middle-aged men dressed in loosely fitted blue robes round it. They barge into the courtyard and walk across it, carrying a long stretcher between them. I recognize the dangling legs immediately—I know their every vein. Dad's legs. The other half of Dad's body is covered with a white bedsheet that's probably too short to hide the rest of his body.

The two men continue hastily walking across the courtyard. They quickly approach a green van and wait for its driver to appear. It's a mortuary van. I didn't notice it before.

I also see that I didn't notice a police cruiser parked on the other edge of the courtyard. It's empty. I look back at the van. Its driver jumps out of his seat and opens the rear doors. Pale blue tattoos on his fingers stretch hideously as he helps the two men lift the stretcher up and slide it inside.

A hiccup rises in my throat. This is it.

In a world of unimaginable sorrow, how will I be able to live without my father?

Goodbye, Daddy. I love you so.

I remain sitting on the bench, watching the van drive back a bit at first, then after turning, head up the driveway to the road above, hauling my father away.

What should I do now? What do I want to do? I think I want to die—no, not die exactly, but I don't want to live either. I lean back onto the bench and close my eyes. Everything turns fuzzy and dark. There's no easier way to die than to fall asleep.

"Laura." Someone's shaking me by the shoulder. "Wake up."

I stare in bafflement at the figure standing in front of me. *Dad?* No. This man is much smaller and wearing a brown suit and a tie; it's not my dad. Besides . . .

"I'm Detective Ivanov," the man informs me. "Your mother asked me to find you."

"Is she in the apartment?" I ask.

"Yes, I'll bring you to her."

He takes me by the hand and leads me to my apartment, as if I don't know where it is. For some reason, I feel light and rested after sleeping, like I've gone to some happy place and spent time there. My throat swells with bitterness. This place I've returned to isn't happy at all.

We find Mom and three police officers in the kitchen. Mom looks surprisingly calm and does everything the policemen tell her to.

One of them, a man who looks more like a teenager, smudges her finger in some black ink, presses it onto a big, official-looking document, then repeats the process with her other fingers.

Sensing my gaze, Mom looks up. "Do you think I did the right thing by killing your father?"

I blink, momentarily thrown by her question. It's so embarrassing. Now everyone's looking at me, waiting for my answer. I'm sure Mom did this on purpose, for her audience. I don't answer and, instead, study the second officer.

His eyes are bloodshot. *Infection? A fight?* He suddenly gets up and lifts Mom's shoes from under the table.

"How do you describe these?" he asks her, staring at the shoes dumbly. If not for the seriousness of the situation, it could've been hilarious.

"Pink jelly sandals," Mom answers expertly.

The officer nods and sits back in the chair to scribble the description in his report.

"Ready to roll?" asks the third police officer, who's been guarding the entrance to the kitchen.

I've never seen a man with long side whiskers in person before, only in movies. He approaches my mother and swiftly handcuffs her wrists.

"I'll stay a while longer," the detective yells out of Dad's room.

As one of the policemen nudges Mom forward, I go closer to her and whisper a question that has been bothering me, "How did you kill Dad?"

"With his axe," she replies. "I beheaded him."

I stagger back, stunned. She had no qualms at all saying it in a loud voice, making the policemen stop simultaneously to look at her in disbelief. They obviously weren't expecting her to tell me this so bluntly. I bite my cheek painfully and walk out the front door, getting ahead of everyone.

A crowd of curious onlookers has already gathered on the porch. I'm bewildered at how fast the news can travel. Putting an indifferent expression on my face, I walk past them and continue toward the courtyard. The neighbors tumble down the pathway after us, filling it with whispers and half-uttered words.

"Why didn't you just divorce your husband?" Mrs. Zorina shouts at Mom in a desperate voice.

Everyone gasps at her audacity. One of the policemen shushes them immediately. Now my neighbors seem to me like a mob of strangers. There's so much anger in their expressions as they watch Mom being escorted toward the police cruiser.

Mom's expression is vacant. She seems to be thrown by the question the woman has asked. This is maybe the first time she's even thought of that option. Or was it ever an option? Maybe she didn't want to live at someone else's house and wanted this apartment all for herself and me.

My mind is burning with different questions, and one of them is very important.

I hurry to the cruiser and ask Mom, "How did the police find out?"

"I went to the station and confessed," she says simply.

Of course, it must have been weighing heavily on her conscience. I wonder why the police didn't arrest her then and there. Maybe they didn't believe her.

"Bring our dogs to Mrs. Volk's house tomorrow," Mom says.

"I can take care of them," I say but then think again. I can find food in dumpsters and do other things to earn some money, but what if they need a vet?

"OK," I say. "They'll probably like the countryside life."

"Don't worry, we'll be millionaires when I return," Mom says in a booming voice so the neighbors will hear her too. "President Gorbachev is our relative."

I wince as everyone starts to laugh. Can't they see my mother is ill? Though I understand their animosity. They adored my dad, who had a golden touch and did all their repairs.

The policeman who looks like a teenager turns to the neighbors and asks, "Can anyone take Laura for the night? We'll send a social worker tomorrow."

"I can," Mrs. Yermol volunteers immediately. "I'm like a grandma to her."

Is she like a grandma to me? Yes, she is.

"Thank you very much," the policeman says, then bows his head respectfully and gets in the cruiser with the other policemen and my mother, who's looking at everyone through the window.

She has a wide smile on her face. It's her protective mask, I think. She wants to pretend all is well.

I wave at her, and we give each other a helpless look. I tear my gaze away and stare instead at the moving cruiser. Like the van did before, it circles the courtyard, then drives toward the road above and disappears from view.

Mrs. Yermol touches my shoulder. "You know that my spare room is currently rented to tourists. Can you sleep in your apartment?"

I whip my head and stare at her, dumbfounded. Did she lie to the police officer when she said she'd take me for the night? She worked as a teacher for heaven's sake; how could she lie?

"Will you?" she asks again.

"No problem," I reply but continue staring at her. *Wow.*

A sudden flash of light jolts me from my stupor. I turn and see a massive camera with a black umbrella over it pointed at me. It clicks again, and I throw an arm over my face, recoiling.

"A reporter," Mrs. Yermol says.

Someone grabs my shoulders from behind and says, "Leave the courtyard."

I dash toward the stairs and jog to my apartment. I pause before the front door and study the number. Taking a deep breath, I open the door and step inside.

Chapter Eighteen
The Loneliest Girl in the World

The apartment is eerily quiet. The lights are turned off. All the doors to the rooms are open. There's a weird, sour smell I haven't noticed before. It's wafting strong in the air. What can it be?

I tentatively cross the corridor and peek inside Dad's room. The furniture stands in its usual place, undisturbed. Nails and screws are scattered on the table around full ashtrays. Dad's rubber boots are half lying in their usual place in the corner of the room. Nothing seems to be out of the ordinary. Except for . . . the couch. The scream freezes in my throat. There's a big puddle of blood on it, at least a bucketful, weighing the left side of the couch down. I step back, cowering.

With my limbs feeling laden, I go to Mom's and my room and sit on my bed. The mattress is bare for some reason. Oh . . . my sheet was used to cover Dad.

For the first time, I allow myself to cry. I rock and rock and wail quietly. Then I feel better, and I hate this. I don't want to be soothed. I want to feel all the pain forever.

Drying the tears from my nose and chin, I go to our small refrigerator and open it. The only food it has is five jars of cured pork fat. Gross, but Mom manages to eat it for energy when there's no other food. I'll have to bring it to her. She must be famished by now.

I get a plastic bag and shove the five jars inside, then change my clothes to casual ones and walk purposefully outside. I'm not going to think of anything anymore.

I stroll along the mostly empty streets, listening to the soft clicking of my shabby yellow shoes and looking down at the tiles that make up the pavement. Do Dad's footprints still linger on them? I'm overwhelmed with the possibility that yes, I can find something here that belonged to Dad. Am I stepping right now where he stepped?

A middle-aged man is dancing barefoot on the road ahead of me. He's blocking traffic and holding his hat out for the drivers to throw some money into it.

My heart jumps as I focus on his face. He looks just like my dad—he has the same silver hair, wide nose, and light blue eyes. Compassion fills my heart. I keep staring at the man with bittersweet greediness, trying to get as much association with Dad as possible. This man is also poor and goofy. I hope he's not homeless and doesn't spend all his money on vodka. But his eyes are just as sad as my dad's when he was drunk.

I make myself turn away. Gawking isn't polite. I continue walking straight ahead. The farther I go, the darker the blue sky becomes. Is Dad up there now or still here? People say that the spirits of the dead stay on earth for forty days and only then move on to the sky.

Time to focus on the task at hand. I look left and right, make sure no cars are close, and quickly cross the road to the painfully familiar police station.

Two police officers are just exiting, and I hurry toward them. "Wait."

Maybe it's because of the uniforms, but many of the policemen I've seen so far are lookalikes: tall and slim with brown hair and stern expressions. I don't remember seeing any policewomen so far.

"Could you pass this bag of food to my mother?" I ask as they stop.

One of the officers steps forward, looking concerned. "What's your mother's last name?"

"Meer. She was arrested earlier today."

"She's in jail then, not at the police station."

"Oh. Is that the one that's near the seaport?"

"Yes."

I say thank you and walk away from the yard, holding my head down, thinking. There's no way the jail will let me in, so I don't need this food anymore. I drop the bag into a trash can nearby and run back home.

Everything is a blur. I can only see colorful maple leaves whirling in the wind, looking withered and sad. It seems even nature is grieving for my father.

My chest hurts from running, and I switch to walking. Where am I hurrying to anyway? Do I really want to be in my apartment and to sleep there? It's just a little bit scary. Maybe I should build a tree house or a hut in Dad's garden and sleep there. Good idea.

As I get closer to our street, a plan for making a hut starts to take shape, becoming clearer and clearer. I climb the street stairs and round the corner, deciding to cut through the two twin buildings.

Suddenly, a neighbor calls out from her porch on the second floor.

"Wait for me, please," she says, peering at me over the railing.

"OK," I reply respectfully. She's the mother of my friends Egor and Ulani, so I even curtsy when she comes downstairs.

"Sorry it took me so much time to walk," she says, her wide chin squeezing into her neck as she looks down at me. "Carrying my extra weight is difficult."

"You're not plump," I protest.

She laughs, then raises her hand and changes her expression to serious. "Did the police officers tell you when they were going to send you to the orphanage?"

"I won't be sent to the orphanage!" I say firmly.

"You don't have any relatives. Of course you will."

"I won't."

"You don't understand, Laura—"

I huff. "I understand perfectly, and I'm telling you I won't be sent to any orphanage."

I stomp away, glad I had the last word. It's the easiest way to win an argument, just by leaving. I can't argue the way my mother does. She can do it forever.

In Dad's garden, I get to a thick tree and break off some of its leafy branches, apologizing profusely in case they can feel pain. I lean the branches vertically against each other until they resemble a tiny house in the shape of a cone. It's complete now.

The branches smell sweet and spicy, incredibly relaxing—just what I need after a day like this. Stepping back, I admire my work. The hut looks cozy, a magical place to live in.

I get on my hands and knees and crawl inside my protective cocoon through a little opening I left, settling comfortably on the soft grass. Perrrrfect!

"What do we have here?" a boy's voice asks from somewhere outside.

I crawl out and look up to see Anthony, another boy I stopped hanging out with because he called me a boy.

Today he looks like he hasn't had a bath for ages; his hair is sticking to his forehead like upturned Christmas trees. Although, who am I to judge?

"What the hell are you doing here?" I ask spitefully.

He smiles maliciously, then turns his head and darts toward my hut, jumping on it with the full force of his body, smashing it completely.

"Oh no!" I yell, feeling my heart breaking for the second time in one day. From the pain. From the hurt. From the unfairness of it all.

Anthony thinks it's hilarious; he's laughing his guts out.

I choke out the words, "I'm going to kick your ass."

He runs away, and I chase him, sprinting into the courtyard. Then Anthony turns and makes a monkey face at me. I don't want to laugh, but I do, loudly and heartily. Ugh, I hate that I forgive people so quickly.

"I'll catch you," I shout through my fit of laughter. "I'll catch you. I'll catch you!"

Suddenly, someone grabs me by the hand from behind and jerks me backward. I cringe in fear, thinking it's Anthony's mother who's going to scold me for chasing her son, but it's not—it's our neighbor, Mrs. Orlova, the TV star. She keeps holding my hand, squeezing it painfully.

"How dare you laugh on such a tragic day!" she shouts, her hollow cheeks quivering.

I can't meet her eyes, so I look down at my ugly shoes. Indeed, why am I laughing? I understand her anger. My dad helped her build her country cottage, and she respected him so much.

"Let her be!" our neighbor, Ms. Iva, speaks up from the other side of the courtyard.

Mrs. Orlova looks at her in stunned silence.

"This girl has had enough misfortune in her life," she says. "She should have all the fun she wants."

Surprisingly, Mrs. Orlova lowers her gaze, looking chastened, but then she looks up at me again and asks quietly, "Just tell me one thing: Do you think your mother did the right thing by murdering your father?"

I look away immediately, hiding my eyes. I decide that I'm not going to answer her truthfully. Mom is the only family member I have left now. I have to protect her.

"Yes," I reply, bending under the weight of my lie.

"Shame on you," she hisses through her smudged-with-purple-lipstick teeth, then drops my hand like I've burned her, staggering away.

I look at Ms. Iva, finding protection in her piercing gaze. Born with some of her fingers missing, she's led a secluded life. But here she is, a sweet older lady who's defended me.

"Are you OK?" she asks, coming to stand by my side.

I nod, and we turn to watch as Mrs. Orlova strides to a Volga, where her driver is waiting for her, holding the rear door open.

"You must be hungry," Ms. Iva says, drawing my attention back to her. "Come, I'll give you the salad I fixed this morning."

I nod and follow her upstairs to the third floor. When we enter her apartment, I look around with curiosity. The rooms are barely furnished, but every surface is gleaming and spotless. All older ladies, I've noticed, like to keep their homes neat and organized.

I also see an impressive collection of porcelain figurines randomly placed around the living room. They represent people of the seventeenth or eighteenth century. Who knew Ms. Iva had this interesting hobby and was a collector? Although many of us like to collect things. I collect chewing gum wrappers, Dad collected rare, expensive bottles, and Mom . . . OK, she doesn't collect anything.

"The kitchen is there," Ms. Iva says, gesturing for me to go in there.

I smile sheepishly at her, then walk over to a soft chair at the table and sit down. I watch Ms. Iva open a very tall fridge, pull out a bowl of salad, then spoon a quarter of it on a flat plate for me. It looks yummy and beautiful.

As she lays the salad in front of me, I examine its many elaborate layers covering the chopped herring. There are grated potatoes, carrots, beets, and eggs. At the top, the masterpiece is decorated with a parsley sprig.

"Here's your fork," Ms. Iva says, putting it on the table next to the bowl. "Enjoy your meal."

She also pours me a glass of apple juice and puts it next to the fork, then she walks over to the window and sits on a little stool there.

I shovel a forkful of salad into my mouth and chew. Delicious. I continue chewing. Finally, I'm eating. All of a sudden, a memory of the odd smell in my apartment comes to my mind. The fish smells almost like that. I grip my stomach with my arm and hunch over, trying not to heave. I have the juice, thankfully. I grab the glass and gulp it down.

Ms. Iva hasn't noticed my less-than-tactful behavior. She's intently staring out the window, lost in thought. I wonder if she intentionally swiveled away on her stool so as not to watch me any longer. It's too much for her, and she instinctively distanced herself from me and my troubles.

"I'm sorry," I say quietly so as not to startle her. "I can't eat."

Ms. Iva turns and nods understandingly. "You can come anytime later."

"OK," I say, standing to my feet. "Are you going to the courtyard now?"

"No, it's getting late. I'll watch TV."

"I can still play with my friends."

"You do just that, dear."

I run out her front door and back downstairs.

"Laura," I hear Polina's voice from somewhere nearby.

"Where are you?" I yell.

"Under the staircase."

I dash to the garden island between the two twin buildings and crouch to dip under the exterior stairs. This place may be a great sleeping spot tonight. A lot of stray cats sleep here too. It's so safe that they even give birth to kittens here. I'll just bring the pillow and blanket from my bed. I did something like that once before, sleeping on the street while waiting for Mom to return from her night shift at the local government building, where she worked as a cleaning lady.

"Mr. Tsvet was looking for you," George says, breaking my train of thought. Oh, he's here too. I look around the tiny, dark space. It's quite a party here. There are George, Ava, Polina, and Olivia.

"Who's Mr. Tsvet?" I ask George.

"Mia's grandfather. He went around the building to continue searching for you."

"Mia's grandfather? I know him. I guess I'll have to go and ask what he wants."

Reluctantly, I leave the group and circle the building, then look for Mr. Tsvet in the courtyard. He's nowhere to be seen, but then I catch a glimpse of him on the street stairs. He's walking down, leaning heavily on his varnished wooden cane. I feel sorry he had to take the stairs because of me.

"I'm here!" I yell, running to him.

He turns and, in a friendly way, says, "There you are!"

"Why were you looking for me?"

"My wife and I are taking you in for the night. Let's go."

I follow him to the apartment building, and we climb the stairs to the fourth floor, where his wife is waiting for us in the doorway, smiling.

"Sweetie," she says, pulling me into a hug.

The endearment breaks something in me, and I begin to sob.

"There, there," she coos, clutching me to her. "Everything is going to be alright."

I try to smile at her, but the skin over my upper lip starts trembling. I press it with my hand and step inside the apartment.

Mrs. Tsvet tightens the hairpins in her white bun, then leads me to a rack full of small shoes—Mia's shoes. What a pity she's already left for Moscow, where her parents live. She stays with her grandparents only for a month during summers. It would be so much fun to live with her and learn things from her, like drawing and whatnot. Once she gave me a painting of a horse she'd made, and it was so realistic that adults couldn't believe she'd done it.

"Choose the ones you like," Mrs. Tsvet says, tapping me on the shoulder.

I choose the slippers that are pink, of course, and slip into them. Then I circle the corridor twice, beaming with pride. I'm wearing something that belongs to a nice girl.

"Wash your hands in the bathroom," Mrs. Tsvet gently commands. "I've already hung a towel for you there. After that, come to the kitchen."

I quickly soap and rinse my hands, then walk out of the bathroom and follow the delicious smell of garlic and freshly cut parsley. My appetite suddenly comes with a vengeance.

I inhale loudly. "Smells good."

Mrs. Tsvet chuckles. "Chicken noodle soup."

She sprinkles it with salt, then ladles it into a bowl and puts it in front of me. She then gives me a plate with crispy crackers.

I start eating quickly, wolfing down the noodles. It makes Mrs. Tsvet chuckle again. What a lovely sound!

"Eat, eat," she says to me, her delicate face full of charm. "I'll make tea with condensed milk for you."

"Do they even go well together?" I ask. "Tea and milk?"

"The British drink tea with milk all the time."

I shrug and slurp the remaining broth from my bowl. The saltiness is yummy. I lean back and study the kitchen. It's simple, with white-and-blue tiles on the walls, a long counter, a double sink, a garbage disposal, and hazelnut-patterned linoleum on the floor.

"I'm glad you liked the soup," Mrs. Tsvet says, swapping the empty bowl for a cup of tea and a saucer.

"Thank you," I say, remembering to be polite like Mia. Although, I've already failed the Mia test by sucking the liquid right out of the bowl. That's considered poor manners.

The milky tea turns out to be quite tasty, like a creamy cake. I sip it slowly with my eyes closed, prolonging the warmth and sweetness in my mouth.

"Want a dry bagel with it?" Mrs. Tsvet asks, adjusting her glasses.

"No," I reply. "But maybe later."

"Tomorrow morning will be OK?"

"Yes. I can help you wash the dishes now." *That's what Mia would say.*

"No, love, go take a bath. I put out PJs for you there."

I hate baths and being wet. Why do I need a bath? I'm not dirty. *Well, I need to be like Mia.*

"Just what I need," I say, getting up from the table.

The bathroom is in the same place as in our apartment. It gives me a sense of déjà vu. The only difference is that we have two bedrooms and a living room, while the Tsvets have only one bedroom and a living room. Some apartments, like Kristen's, have only a living room and no bedrooms.

I step into the bathroom and lock the door. Unlike the lock on our bathroom door, this one works. I go to the two faucets and twist both of them, mixing the water into a nice, almost hot spray.

I stand by the tub, waiting for it to fill up, then climb into the embracing warm water. How could I ever have disliked baths? The heaviness makes me sleepy. I don't want to ever get out.

"Are you OK?" Mrs. Tsvet calls from the other side of the door after I've been in the bath for more than an hour.

"Yes," I reply lazily.

With no enthusiasm, I climb out of the tub, step into my new slippers, and rub my body with the towel. The PJs draped over the radiator are covered in pandas. *Mia's too.* I put them on, marveling at how heavenly soft the material feels. But it also feels like I don't belong in such nice clothes.

Mr. and Mrs. Tsvet are watching TV in the living room when I come out of the bathroom. I walk in tentatively, and Mrs. Tsvet pats the sofa for me to sit next to her. As I do, she picks up a comb and starts raking it through my wet hair.

"Poor kid has lice," Mrs. Tsvet mutters under her breath.

"No way!" I say. "It hasn't itched since forever."

"They're there."

"OK. I can get kerosene from my apartment tomorrow and apply it to my hair."

"No, we'll buy you a special shampoo from a pharmacy."

She finishes combing my hair and braids it into two braids. My hair has grown a lot over the summer. No one will say I look like a boy now.

"Eight o'clock," Mrs. Tsvet announces. "Time for bed."

My eyebrows shoot up to my forehead. Even toddlers go to bed at nine after they watch the children's TV program *Good Night, Little Ones* with Stepashka the Hare and Khryusha the Piglet.

As Mrs. Tsvet shows me my bed in the adjacent room, it occurs to me that she and her husband sleep on the sofa in the living room. The only bed in the house is here, in Mia's room. The room is all about girly design. Paper hearts are glued to the wall around a large nonworking clock, children's books are on the shelves, and colorful artificial flowers are on the tables.

"Good night, Laura," Mrs. Tsvet says. "Would you like me to read you a bedtime story?"

I shake my head.

"Would you like us to say a prayer together?"

I think for a moment, then shake my head again.

She smiles. "A hug then?"

I cock my head. No one has ever offered me this. It seems very nice, but no, I don't want it now.

Mrs. Tsvet smiles again, guessing my answer, but she doesn't seem offended at all, thankfully.

"Good night, sleep tight," she says cheerfully, exiting the room.

"Night-night, don't let the bedbugs bite," I reply and flip the light switch off.

I go to the bed at the wall and lie down. The mattress is wide, thick, and puffy. If I could have such a comfortable bed,

I wouldn't want to be apart from it. I shouldn't get used to it, I know. *It's all temporary and will be gone soon.*

"Laura is doing remarkably well," I hear Mrs. Tsvet say to Mr. Tsvet.

Remarkably well?

"An exceptionally strong kid to go through so much," Mr. Tsvet says.

Strong? Me? I think for a moment and decide that yes, I am strong. Feeling proud of myself, I tug the quilt under my chin and look at the shadows on the ceiling, trying to fall asleep. But sleep doesn't come for a long time. I have difficulty keeping the sad thoughts away. And now there are scary noises in the room, as if someone's thrumming on the windows, trying to break them and get to me . . . get me.

My heart starts pounding. There are other sounds too: the door rattling, the furniture creaking, the walls popping, the ceiling clicking . . . *I don't want to die!* Mercifully, sleep finally comes.

Chapter Nineteen
Responsible Adults

The next day I wake up smiling at the midday sun warming my face. I pull my arms from under the quilt and stretch. Such an incredible sensation.

I look around in confusion. Why don't I recognize the room? The horrible memories of yesterday crash over me. *My dad isn't alive anymore.* I'm all alone now.

Hmm, I need to find our dogs and take them to the tea plantation. I won't tell the Tsvets about my plans, as they won't allow me to go.

Throwing the quilt off, I grab my blouse and put it on, fumbling with the buttons, trying to get dressed quickly. Mia's house slippers will have to do for my walk outside.

I quietly go to the door and press my ear to it. The voices of the Tsvets are coming from the kitchen, I'm sure. It's safe to step out. Softly pulling the door open, I tiptoe into the living room, then leap past the kitchen toward the deadbolt. Sliding it open, I dart outside. Success!

I run downstairs and burst into my apartment. Yesterday I left the door ajar so the dogs could get in. I hoped they'd be inside, but they're not. As I walk into the kitchen, however, and look through the window, I see them lying in Dad's garden, basking in the sun.

I hurry out and walk quickly around the house. "Doll, Mickey!"

They trot toward me, wriggling their backs in a merry dog dance.

"Good girl, good boy," I coo. "Let's go on a journey to the countryside."

Obediently, they follow me down the hill to the main road, where the three of us stop at the intersection to wait for the traffic to clear.

Out of the blue, a police truck turns around on the two-lane road and drives over to where we're standing. I stare at it in confusion.

"Laura, get in," Mom shouts from it.

My mother! I grab the dogs and climb into the back seat next to her. I start kissing her on the cheeks, shocking her. I've never done this before. I give her at least a hundred kisses.

I release the dogs so they can sit in her lap, then ask, "How?"

"The officers here kindly agreed to take our dogs to the tea plantation," she explains.

"That's amazing! And what a coincidence I was on the road."

"As always, you know where to pop up."

I laugh. The truck starts moving, and I take some time to examine the two policemen in the front seats. They're not the ones I saw yesterday, but they look like part of the police brotherhood too: tall, slim, and with brown hair.

The truck's interior is very unusual. The back compartment, where Mom and I are sitting, has sideways seats and only one small window on the back wall. It's surrounded by metal bars; no criminals could escape this place—it's a miniature jail cell.

I shift to look outside through the windshield. The people walking on the streets seem so untroubled and carefree. They don't have any idea of the horrors we're living through. Much to my dismay, I can't remember the feeling I had when everything was in its usual, albeit weird, order. Everyone was alive. Why can't people always be alive? But on the other hand, why are we alive?

"Do you know how humans were created?" I ask Mom.

For the first time, she doesn't blurt out an answer. Instead, she sits still, thinking it over. I'm surprised because she likes to pretend to know it all.

"No," she replies eventually, looking shocked that she doesn't have an opinion on this.

"I know," I lie, just to impress her.

"How?" she asks excitedly.

"By God."

Mom's eyes glaze into a blank stare. She looks disappointed at first but then mulls my answer over. A few seconds later, her expression changes again. She's already dismissed my theory as untrue and is thinking of her own things.

The truck is tracing along the S-curves up the mountain. Mom holds on to the dogs tightly so they won't fall out of her lap. Soon enough, we drive past Mrs. Volk's house, and Mom directs the police officer at the wheel toward the driveway.

He rolls the truck to a stop and says to me, "Wait here."

I still exit the truck with everyone but stay near it as everyone starts walking along the dust-covered driveway. Now I notice that the driver's partner has a touch of gray at his temples. But how? He looks to be in his late twenties.

There's a tree nearby, full of green apples. I decide to climb it. When at the top, I watch Mom and the policemen knock on the door. The only ones who know I'm in the tree are the dogs; they keep glancing at me curiously. I wave at them, then smile sadly.

Why didn't the officers allow me to come with them? I'm beginning to suspect the dogs weren't the only reason we drove here. Oh, they want to question Mrs. Volk. The poor woman knows nothing.

After Mrs. Volk opens the door and everyone goes inside, I turn my attention to the apples. I pick one after another and bite into them, thinking about possible scenarios for my future life. I'm sure the policemen will let Mom go soon, maybe in a month. Meanwhile, I'll just live with the Tsvets.

The door opens again about twenty minutes later, and the two policemen and Mom come out on the porch. I pick the three biggest apples from the top branches and climb down, then hand them to the group.

The policemen surprisingly linger outside the truck and talk to us while eating their apples. The driver chews his apple down to its core, where there are a lot of seeds.

"That good?" I ask him.

"I don't remember the last time I ate fruit straight from the tree," he answers. "It was probably when we had our garden while growing up."

"'We'?"

"My little brothers and I."

"That sounds like a great memory," his partner says, patting him on the shoulder.

"These are your things and clothes," Mom tells me, handing me a plastic bag.

"Oh, great that you brought them," I say appreciatively.

All of us get back into the truck, then we wait for a herd of cows to pass in front of us before the driver pulls away from the driveway, laughing.

I busy myself with looking at cliffs and canyons and counting maple trees. Everything is going by at a fast pace. I close my eyes and quietly sing songs I compose in my head.

Absorbed in my thoughts, I don't notice when the truck comes to a sudden stop at the foot of our street stairs. I straighten up and, after giving my mother's hand a squeeze, climb out.

"Take care," the policeman in the passenger seat says.

"I will," I reply, and a second later, the engine roars to life, and the truck disappears in the direction of the jail.

I reassure myself that everything will be alright, just like Mrs. Tsvet said. Mom will definitely be back soon, and we'll have a nice, easy life.

Will I be in trouble with the Tsvets for leaving without telling them? How can I return to them? I feel so ashamed. The only thing I can do now is pretend I'm the stupidest person in the world and don't understand the rules of good behavior. I'll tell them I always leave home first thing in the morning, telling no one. That's kinda true.

"I was waiting for you," a neighbor standing on the porch near my entrance hall tells me. Everyone wants to talk to me nowadays. Argh! But she's the grandma of one of the small boys I often play with, so I should be nice to her.

"What did you want?" I ask.

"I have an offer for you. If you agree, I can become your grandmother and live with you in your apartment."

I frown. She's never talked to me before, and now she wants to be my grandma. She doesn't even look like a grandma—her hair is long, hanging over her shoulders, not gray at all.

"I'm listening," I say.

She sighs. "To be honest, I want to live apart from my son and daughter-in-law. I feel like I'm in their way."

I look away, feeling a pang of compassion for her. It must be horrible to live with a family that doesn't want you and to hide in the corners. But do I wanna be a way of escape for her? This new scenario for my future seems appealing, but will she love me or even like me or only pretend to? What if her son begs her to come back? What if she starts hating me? I don't trust her.

"Would you consider it?" she asks as I start walking upstairs.

"I'll think about it," I lie, hoping she won't stop me. She doesn't, and I breathe a sigh of relief.

On the fourth floor, I lift my hand to ring the bell at the Tsvets' apartment, but the door swooshes open before I can press the button.

"Where have you been?" Mrs. Tsvet cries out, sounding distraught. Has she been crying? Her eyes look puffy.

A nervous giggle escapes my lips. No one has ever worried about me like this before. This is silly and mind-boggling.

"I . . . I went to the Matsestinskaya tea plantation with Mom and the police," I say, looking anywhere but at her.

"Why didn't you tell me?" she cries out again. "I've been worried sick."

I shrug, then mumble, "I won't do it again."

Mrs. Tsvet touches her pale cheeks and steps aside to let me in. I go to the bathroom and wash my hands. A dozen or more new mosquito bites are on my arms. The itching will be bad. I should avoid scratching them.

Wiping my hands on the towel, I pause at the mirror and search for signs that something has changed in my face since my dad died. I feel like I'm forty years old. But no, I'm still ten.

Mrs. Tsvet is doing chores in the kitchen. I go to the window there and bend to smell some purple flowers growing in small pots on the sill.

"Violets," Mrs. Tsvet says.

"Plants love me," I boast. "If you want them to grow well, ask me to water them."

"What a nice thing to offer. Do it in four days."

"I'll go write it down."

I head for my bedroom, past Mr. Tsvet, hoping he won't say anything to me about my morning escapade. He doesn't, and I freely slip into the room, then close the door behind me.

I sit at the table and draw a timetable, then put in my daily activities. *Plants on Monday. Homework Monday through Friday. The courtyard every day. A bath . . . every day too?*

I return to the kitchen, finding Mrs. Tsvet deeply engrossed in her task. She's rubbing black pepper and salt into the skin of a whole chicken. I don't remember Mom ever preparing chicken at all, not even pieces of it. The Tsvets must be rich.

"Are you rich?" I ask bluntly.

"Not at all." Mrs. Tsvet gurgles with laughter, as if I've asked the most ridiculous question. "Why would you think that?"

"Your food. We never had a whole chicken at our home."

"If your dad hadn't been drinking, you would have been much richer than we are."

"Do you really think so?"

"Of course! Your dad was a healthy and capable man, and we only have our pensions to rely on. Although, my husband's pension is higher than the average because he worked as a general."

"I saw the picture of him in the living room," I say. "In a green uniform with golden stars."

She smiles.

"And I saw a picture of you very young," I continue. "You had a long braid hanging over your shoulder."

She giggles. "Long braids were in fashion. You know what, let's talk about your dad. Tell me some funny stories about him."

"OK. Let me think . . . He once searched for one of his slippers for two minutes, swearing and cursing, but it was on his foot all along."

Mrs. Tsvet bursts out laughing, and the sound draws Mr. Tsvet into the kitchen.

"Just like my wife," he says, sitting next to me at the table. "She searched for her glasses while they were on her nose."

"Oh, Steven, stop," Mrs. Tsvet protests.

I laugh. "But shouldn't it have been a clue that you could still see while you were searching?"

Her eyes widen. "Look at you, so smart."

I glance sideways at Mr. Tsvet. Isn't he angry with me at all for leaving the apartment? It seems not.

"When is your birthday, Laura?" he asks.

"April twentieth. Why?" Does he want to give me a present? I still want a toy piano. And now that I think of it, will the police give me the money that was in Mom's wallet?

"You don't say!" Mr. Tsvet exclaims, jolting me back from my thoughts. "Mine is too."

"Seriously?"

"Yes. This is a good day for a birthday. A lot of great people were born on this day, except for Hitler—he was a demonic figure in the history of the world."

I nod but think mostly of the coincidence that Mr. Tsvet and I have birthdays on the same day. It makes me feel somehow related to him.

We continue chatting for another twenty minutes until the smell of the baking chicken becomes overwhelming. Mrs. Tsvet takes the sheet pan out of the oven and cuts the chicken into big, crispy chunks. Instructing us not to talk so we won't choke, she lays our plates out on the table and takes a seat to eat with us.

I swallow in anticipation before picking up the crispiest of the wings. The taste is even better than the smell and sight. It'll be my favorite food from now on, together with fried potatoes.

"Tea with crackers?" Mrs. Tsvet asks after she clears the table.

"Yes, please," I reply.

The Tsvets treat me like a princess for the rest of the day, and I love the attention. When the evening comes, I go to my bedroom, sit at the table, and copy Mia's drawings of flowers. When I'm unable to keep my eyes open anymore, I walk over to the bed and plop on the quilt.

Whispering good night to Dad in heaven, I turn on my side and fall asleep.

Chapter Twenty
A Superhero of My Own

My life is so different now that I'm living with the Tsvets. I wake up at the same time every morning, have breakfast, and put on ironed clothes, then Mrs. Tsvet styles my hair for school, and off I go. Sometimes, Mr. Tsvet even drives me in his cute yellow Zaporogec, which looks like a smiling toy.

My classmates know something has changed. They tried to ask me where my father was, but I lied to them that he was at home, safe and sound, thank you very much.

Today, Mrs. Tsvet is on the balcony, mending holes in my clothes. There's a lot of light here, and I help her thread the needle from time to time.

At the moment, I'm standing by the window, watching the courtyard from up high. I've dreamed of doing this for so many years, envying the kids who lived on the top floors. And here I am! I can even imagine I'm flying on a plane.

The doorbell interrupts my reveries, and I jump into the living room, dashing to the front door. It might be my friends. I've already done my homework and am free to go outside to play.

"Don't open the door until you know who's outside," Mr. Tsvet says sensibly, struggling to catch up with me.

I step aside politely and wait for him to look through the peephole. I wish the door in my own apartment had had a peephole and a doorbell too.

"Who's there?" Mr. Tsvet asks.

"Mr. Chaika," a male voice answers. "A police officer from the Child Protective Unit."

Mr. Tsvet unlocks the door immediately, and we look at the tall, muscular, dark-haired man, slightly resembling Sylvester Stallone, standing on the other side of the doorway. He's dressed not in a uniform but in a casual shirt adorned with a big golden eagle.

"Please come in," Mr. Tsvet tells him curtly. "We were expecting you."

Mr. Chaika examines us cooly, then follows Mr. Tsvet into the living room. The two of them take seats in the chairs by the table, stare at each other intently at first, then start to talk. I can hear only bits and pieces.

I edge closer and sit on the sofa, pretending to be interested in the newspaper lying there.

"Let me be frank with you," Mr. Chaika says. "Laura needs a foster family, and you'd be a perfect choice for her."

"Let me be frank with you as well," Mr. Tsvet says. "I'm a dying man. The doctors gave me only a few months to live."

What? No!

Mr. Chaika continues to stare at him impassively, assessing, not believing, I think. But I believe Mr. Tsvet. Poor man! Can't he be cured?

I shift my gaze to the floor. Mr. Chaika is studying me now. Why am I avoiding his eyes? I look back up and stare straight at him. He smiles at me kindly, then sighs.

"Can I use your phone to call my wife?" he asks Mr. Tsvet.

"Yes, of course," Mr. Tsvet replies.

Mr. Chaika stands up and goes to the phone, then dials the numbers with quick, practiced movements of his finger. In addition to a peephole and doorbell, I now also want a telephone back at my apartment. I remember Dad saying that it would cost him a year's wages to install one, so it's very expensive.

"Talia, hi," Mr. Chaika says into the receiver, turning his back to me. *Talia? My mother's name?*

"You're still home, good," he continues. "Would you mind me bringing a ten-year-old girl to live with us?"

My heart flutters. *He wants to take me in?*

What I'd give to hear what his wife is answering. Mr. Chaika listens carefully, giving nothing away, then replies, "If we have two beds for our children, we'll certainly find another one for her."

Oh, his wife doesn't want me. Egor and Ulani's mom was right—I'll end up in an orphanage. It's so scary. I've heard some terrifying stories about orphanages and about adults turning into monsters there. I even once knew a young lady who'd grown up in an orphanage, and almost all her teeth were gone. I can't imagine what happened to her.

"Understood," Mr. Chaika says. "Be careful on your trip."

He hangs up the phone, then turns to Mr. Tsvet. "Let's pack Laura's things. I'll call a friend to pick us up."

"Yes, sir," Mr. Tsvet replies and gestures for Mrs. Tsvet, who's been listening in the doorway, to start the packing.

"Most of my things are in my apartment," I chime in.

"We'll go there," Mr. Chaika says with a nod.

After Mrs. Tsvet is done gathering my things into two big bags, we proceed downstairs.

In my apartment, I collect only my clothes and leave my toys in Mom's and my room. Mr. Chaika told me we'll come back to get them later. I hide my Barbie in the top drawer and go into Dad's room.

I don't really need anything here. I just want to look at Dad's things. I pretend to search for something in his closet, where the air still holds his *alive* smell. Dad's clothes are hanging neatly in a tight row. One jacket is quite stylish and colorful, though I never saw Dad wear it.

For a second, I wonder if he didn't really die. Wishful thinking, I know. I had a dream recently that Dad was standing in this room, explaining to me that he'd just been in a hospital, healing from brain trauma, and now he was back. I woke up from that dream crying with relief, then I started crying in disappointment as reality set in. He would never come back. The thought was crushing.

Mr. Tsvet and Mr. Chaika are examining Dad's glass sideboard with his beautiful collection of brightly colored liquor and rum bottles. There are Malibu, Blue Curaçao, Kiwi Wonder, Banana Bolse, and so on. Dad found all these bottles on the beach—empty, of course. In reality, he could afford only vodka, cheap wine, and occasionally champagne. I didn't like him drinking red wine, because his lips would resemble a vampire's afterward.

"Come on, Laura," Mr. Chaika says, urging me to hurry.

Did he see the pool of blood on the couch? It's burgundy now and looks gooey. I whip my head, pretending to see it for the first time.

"Aaah!" I scream half-heartedly.

Mr. Chaika doesn't look impressed. "Let's go."

I follow him out of the apartment, wondering if anyone's ever going to clean Dad's room.

Mrs. Tsvet takes my hand, and all of us go to the courtyard, where some of the neighbor ladies are sitting on the bench, happy to have us as entertainment. Among them is Mrs. Yermol, smiling at us like an angel, pretending. I'm sure she has no guilt that she didn't take me in.

At that moment, a friend of Mr. Chaika's pulls over to the side of the courtyard in a small white car. He gets out and helps Mr. Chaika put my things in the trunk.

"Be happy, dear," Mrs. Tsvet tells me, drawing me into a hug. "Come visit us as often as you want."

"I will," I say, giggling in embarrassment.

Mr. Chaika helps me get into the back seat of the car and fastens a seatbelt across my chest. Jeez, he's so serious—too serious.

The noisy engine sputters, and it's my cue to wave at everyone through the window. How long will I be gone? A month? Two? Three? I'll try to find ways to make the time pass quickly. Adventures, adventures are waiting for me.

About ten minutes later, we arrive at a courtyard that seems painfully familiar. I've played here so many times with the son of one of Mom's colleagues who lives here. This place has too many tall trees, and they block the sunlight. I don't like that, because the absence of the sun makes me feel sad, big-time. On the bright side, this courtyard has an adjacent basketball court that holds a lot of possibilities for my future games.

I get out of the car and swagger past two girls, who look at me curiously. I pretend not to see them at all and only watch Mr. Chaika's back as he walks into the tiny entrance hall of a three-story building, then continues upstairs.

I shadow him quietly, wondering which door is going to be the one. We stop at the metal door of apartment number five on the second floor, and Mr. Chaika produces a giant key.

"Uh . . . when are you taking me to the orphanage?" I ask as he lets us inside.

"You want to go to the orphanage?" he asks, his eyes twinkling.

"No," I answer earnestly.

"Then you'll stay with us."

Suddenly, a door on our left flings open, and a ginger-haired boy about my age jumps out into the corridor. "Hi, I'm Leo! I'm nine."

He's wearing only white cotton briefs. I hold in a snort of laughter and say in a high-pitched, girly voice, "Hello, my name is Laura. I'm ten years old."

"Would you like to see my toys?" he asks, with no preamble whatsoever.

"Yes. How many do you have?"

"A whole cabinet."

"That's astounding," I say, using a clever word.

"Yes, it is."

I follow him to the room from which he jumped out and sit on the couch, watching him go to a wide cabinet by the wall and open one of its doors. This room isn't Leo's room; it's a living room.

He dumps out all the cabinet's contents onto the carpet. Impressive! A dozen toys bounce helter-skelter. There's even a PlayStation.

I immediately start thinking of my own toys left behind at my apartment. I need to go there as soon as possible to retrieve them. Why didn't I stash at least Barbie in one of the bags?

"What grades do you usually get in school?" Leo asks me.

"Only straight As," I reply, deadpan.

"Are you an A student?" he asks excitedly, looking impressed.

I giggle. "No. I bring As home only because I scratch out the other grades from my school report card."

His face falls, and he looks disgusted. I wait for the humor to hit him, but it doesn't.

"Scratching out grades won't work now that you and I are classmates," he says.

"We are?" I ask, surprised.

"Yes."

"So you're going to be snitching on me? Where I come from, we don't tattle on each other."

He thinks for a second. "OK, maybe not."

"I was kidding about scratching out my grades, you know," I tell him. "My parents never checked my report card. So . . . and . . . are you an A student?"

"No, but I'm in love with one."

"Are you now?" I chuckle. "Is she pretty?"

He nods vigorously. "And she's a ballerina. Everyone else is in love with her too."

I immediately feel envious. No one has ever been in love with me.

Leo piles his toys at my feet, and I slide down on the floor to examine them. My thoughts, however, are still with the ballerina.

"Is she our classmate?" I ask.

"Yes," Leo answers. "But maybe . . . I should fall in love with you so she'll become jealous. Ha!"

He laughs like a hyena, and I think there's no way he'll manage to make the ballerina jealous, especially by falling in love with me.

The orange carpet in the room is sturdy but comfortable. I realize we never had one back at home, only on a wall in our spare bedroom for decoration and warmth.

Leo touches my hand. "Look at this toy."

"Red binoculars?" I ask.

"No, silly—View-Master. You can look at images through it."

I take the thing from the floor and look inside. It's almost like my kaleidoscope, only better.

"What are your other interests besides toys?" I ask curiously.

"The Italian Mafia," he answers and pauses for effect.

"What?" I screech. "Get out!"

He smiles mysteriously, his eyes wide. "I'm serious. I wanna be a part of it."

"You watch too many movies."

He shrugs and goes back to playing with his toys.

"So, what's the name of the ballerina?" I ask, still hung up on the thought of her.

"Hana," Leo replies absentmindedly.

I sigh and take a few minutes to examine the living room further. There's a glass cabinet filled with old books that are probably boring. I wonder if the Chaikas really read them or just keep them there for show.

Everything in the room is in order, hidden in cabinets and drawers. The wallpaper is light and glossy. There's a music player with disco lights sitting on the TV set. I'd sure love to use it for my dancing and singing when no one's at home.

The ceiling is much higher than the one in my apartment, and it makes it feel like it's easier to breathe here.

I get up and go to the open door of the adjacent room to take a peek inside. Mr. and Mrs. Chaika's bedroom, I guess. There's a vanity for makeup, a big bed, and a tall cabinet with rows and rows of soccer balls on top. They're all autographed. By the super stars of soccer?

"Why do you have so many balls?" I ask Leo.

"My dad is the president of the soccer federation," he replies proudly. "But it's a hobby, not his job."

"If I could whistle, I would," I quip.

"Prepare to watch lots of soccer games. You won't be whistling then. They drive Mom crazy."

"Wow, no, I won't like that, but I'll find something else to do. Do you have a deck of cards for me?"

The door to the living room suddenly opens, and a big, colorful dog runs inside, with Mr. Chaika following it. I kneel and let the dog sniff me. It looks like a huge fox with a sharp nose and smiling mouth. He's almost as big as a Saint Bernard, the dog of my dreams.

"His name is King," Mr. Chaika tells me. "He's a collie."

"A collie," I repeat.

King's long fur is rough to the touch, but it's very beautiful, all shades of red and ginger, plus white on the neck.

"Who drank the can of condensed milk that was in the fridge?" Mr. Chaika asks, pointedly looking at Leo.

"I," Leo says, sucking his lip through a gap in his front teeth.

"So the saying 'He who doesn't work, neither shall he eat' is wrong then? Should it be 'He who works, neither shall he eat'?"

Leo giggles. "Probably."

I laugh too and resume playing with Leo's toys.

When the evening comes, I also meet Mr. Chaika's parents. His father greets me curtly, then disappears into one of the other rooms in the apartment, but his mother stays, staring at me with her hawkish eyes. It seems like she disapproves of her son's decision to bring me here. Oh well, whatever. I try not to look back at her so I won't flinch. However, her eyes suck me right back in.

When she finally leaves the room, I turn to Leo. "What does she do?"

"She works as a cook at the tuberculosis hospital," he answers.

"Spooky, lots of people die from that illness. I heard some people even eat dogs to get better. I'd rather die than do that."

"That's just a rumor," Leo says, relieving my fears.

"And what does your grandfather do?"

"Gramps is a retired ambulance driver."

"Do they like working with sick people?" I ask.

"No, it's just that we live next to the hospital area. All the hospitals stand there in a cluster. First, you're born in a hospital, and then . . ."

"Then you end up in a cemetery that's just one bus stop away," I joke.

"The cemetery is next to the children's hospital, so there are no bus stops between them."

This conversation is going out of whack. I change the subject. "Your grandfather looks like the bear from the cartoon Mashenka and the Bear."

Leo bursts out laughing. "I'm going to tell him that."

"Please don't. He'll think I meant he was fat."

Suddenly, Leo jumps from his seat and yells, "Varvara!"

I look up, and there's another member of the family, a young woman with long, silky black hair.

"This is my sister," Leo says to me.

Varvara is wearing high heels and looks like an adult. She hugs Leo, then looks at me. "Hi, Laura. Dad just told me about you. It's so cool you're going to live with us. How are you?"

"Fine, thank you," I reply politely, trying to make a good first impression. "What have you been doing all day?"

She tosses her hair from her shoulder and chuckles. "College till 3 p.m., then I hung out with my friends at a café in the trade gallery alley."

"Oh, that's just a road away from where I lived."

Her eyes widen. "Wouldn't it be great to wake up fifteen minutes before work? I mean, in summers I help my mother to sell clothes in her shops there."

"I helped my dad sell things too. I'd like to help your mother with that. Where is she, by the way?"

Leo answers instead of Varvara. "On a business trip to Syria. She'll bring us lots of foreign candies and other sweet treats. You'll like it."

My mouth starts to water. Oh my, I'm going to be in paradise.

"Let's take King for a walk," Varvara offers, and we gleefully yell yes.

King is barking gleefully too. He knows the word "walk." It'll never stop amazing me how clever dogs are.

Varvara unlocks the front door, and we all file out after her and go downstairs. Once outside, Leo finds a thick stick, and we start throwing it for King to fetch. He thoroughly enjoys running back and forth across the basketball court, again and again.

"Time to go home," Varvara announces after thirty minutes.

I realize she is still in her fashionable high heels. Everything she's wearing is stylish. It's like she's playing with dolls, only her doll is she herself. Today the Varvara doll is dressed in a puffy-sleeved blouse and black leather pants. I wonder what she'll wear tomorrow.

"How old are you?" I ask her.

"Nineteen," she answers.

"Wow, I wish I were nineteen."

When we get home, Varvara leads us to the bathroom to wash our hands, then goes to help her grandmother unfold the dining table and set dinner on it.

All of us except Mr. Chaika Sr. sit around the table, ready to eat. I make a face of disgust as I see the food loaded with boiled onions. How will I be able to eat this? I'd better only drink the juice made of feijoa jam.

No such luck. Everyone turns their heads to look at me expectantly, waiting for me to start eating with them. I smile wryly and take the bowl with mashed potatoes, scoop a few spoonfuls on my plate, then start the elaborate job of fishing out the onions.

Mrs. Chaika Sr.'s eyes widen as I drop the pieces on the table. Her false teeth start clicking.

"What?" I ask, raising my left eyebrow—the only one I can move independently. "I don't like onions."

"No man will ever marry you," she grumbles. "Because you won't add any onions to the dishes you cook."

"Meh, as if someone will want to marry me," I say and continue pushing my fork through the potatoes.

Surprisingly, they turn out to be delicious—milky and buttery and salty.

After dinner, Mrs. Chaika Sr. stops me from leaving the table and orders me to take all the plates to the kitchen sink to wash them.

Begrudgingly, I do as I'm told and end up enjoying my alone time. It's peaceful and liberating. I can relax my face from all expressions and be myself.

After sliding the washed dishes into a drying rack, I clean up the kitchen counters and make myself a cup of sugary tea. Slowly sipping from the cup, I go stand by the window.

The evening light is disappearing, but a lot of people are still hurrying home along the street, probably returning from work. How's Mom, I wonder? *How's Dad?*

Eventually I return to the living room, and Mr. Chaika comes from his bedroom to show me the gray couch where

I'm going to be sleeping. He also shows me two other couches where Varvara and Leo sleep. The black couch where I sat earlier today actually belongs to Varvara. And Leo's red couch looks more like a giant, overstuffed armchair.

My couch is in the corner of the room, near the TV set and closest to the balcony. I'll enjoy looking through its glazed windows.

I cross the room and sit down on my new couch. Very cozy. I like it.

"I added a chair to it so a long mattress would fit," Mr. Chaika says. "You're very tall. Varvara will show you later where your pillow and blanket are."

We watch TV for the next hour, and my eyes grow strained from looking at the screen at an angle. I grab my notebook and busy myself with doodling in it. I fill one page up with scribbles, tear it from the notebook, crumple it into a ball, then drop it on the floor. I repeat the process with the second page and the third and the next, hoping to draw something beautiful, but it all turns out to be like crap. I can't stand it. I tear out another page and throw it out of my sight.

"Stop it," Varvara says firmly but gently.

Feeling chastened, I bend down to pick up the paper balls, then go to the kitchen to dispose of them. I seize the moment again and stand at the window, looking at the street below. I notice for the first time the recycling center booth on the other side of the tree-lined sidewalk where Dad and I sometimes sold our empty bottles. If only he knew that one day I'd end up living just across the street.

When I return to the room, Varvara tells us to prepare for bedtime. She shows me the closet with my bedding and pillow, and I grab them, dumping them over my couch and chair.

Lying down, I pull the woolen blanket up to my neck and turn to watch Varvara click off the lights and grope her way to her couch. The resulting darkness is creepy. I bury my head in the blanket and distract myself by singing under my breath. If I cover my ears, then only I can hear what I'm singing. I don't understand the words of the Spanish theme song from *The Rich Also Cry*, but I like the way the language sounds.

"We're trying to sleep here, Laura," Leo snaps, and I hear him throw his pillow over his head.

I freeze. They can hear it? But how? Mom never heard me when I sang like this. *Or did she?* A hiccup of embarrassment rises in my throat. I stop breathing, not daring even to shift. One second, two, three . . . my mind starts rolling down a slope—I'm falling asleep.

Suddenly, an audible pop jerks me back into consciousness. I heard a metal jar bouncing on the asphalt. I clearly heard it! Was it in my head? Was I hallucinating? The only thing that scares me more is becoming a drunkard like my dad was. I'll never try even a sip of alcohol. That's when the addiction can sneak up on you.

Chapter Twenty-One
Scary Illusions

I wake up in the morning and feel that my throat is dry and sore. I swallow painfully and decide to ignore it. A cherry tree on the other side of the balcony windows is swaying in a light breeze like a dancer. Breeze or not, it's going to be a very warm day—the sun is already out.

"Hurry up and get dressed for school," Leo grumbles.

I'm usually too cranky for cheery conversations in the mornings—even more so now that I'm under the weather. I want to snap at Leo but restrain myself.

"School satchels aren't cool anymore," Leo says as I grab mine from the closet where Mr. Chaika put all my things. "I'll give you one of my old backpacks."

"OK with me," I say. *Be a nice girl, Laura, say thank you.* "Thank you."

My clothes are perfect. Mrs. Tsvet gave me Mia's white top with a zipper and short jean skirt. Jean-everything is all the rage nowadays. And . . . I truly like the orange backpack Leo hands me.

"Don't you have school clothes?" he grumbles disapprovingly.

Ugh, I can only be nice for so long.

"Let me be," I snap.

He looks at me, hurt, I think, then shrugs and nudges me out the door. "Only fifteen minutes till the first class starts."

As we walk down the street to school, we give each other the silent treatment, and I have plenty of time for my anxious thoughts. Will my classmates like me? Will I be a good student after missing practically all elementary school?

"Gramps gave me pocket money and not you," Leo suddenly brags.

Is he trying another tack after he failed to get a rise out of me earlier?

"Who am I to your gramps?" I ask. "Why should he give me money?"

Leo raises his eyebrows. "That's harsh."

"Harsh or not, what do I need money for? Doesn't your school have free lunches?"

"Not anymore. Something about no budget."

"The same happened in my previous school," I say, then change the subject. "Do you have a best friend in your class?"

"A few, actually."

"Are the girls in our class nice?"

"Nice." Leo looks at me sideways, not understanding why I even had to ask.

"Are there any bullies at all?"

"What are bullies?"

Is he serious? "People who throw punches or insults at you."

He chortles. "No one will dare bother you since I'm almost your brother."

I stifle the smile that's threatening to creep up my face. To have a brother, a protector, has always been my dream.

We stride into a garden alley leading to the porch of my new school. I scan the vast building ahead. It's similar to my old school, except for a gable rooftop and a bridge-like connection to an adjacent building.

Leo ushers me toward a group of students standing to the side of the main entrance. I square my shoulders and, yet again, put on a pleasant face with a wide smile.

I'm barraged with questions about my previous street, school, hobbies, friends, and so on. Then the girls separate me from the boys and start asking me questions about Leo. I dismiss my first suspicion that they all are in love with him and assign their questions simply to their curiosity. It just can't be true.

Leo was right that my new classmates are nice. They're now sweeping me into the school's lobby and pulling me along to the second floor, where our homeroom supposedly is.

"Where were you born?" a girl with a thick ponytail asks. It's so big that it should be called a horsetail.

"Here, in Sochi," I answer, wishing I had some exotic answer instead.

"Do you know any fun games?"

"I'll show you one tomorrow. I'll create a fun notebook with questionnaires that ask questions like what your favorite color is, what boys you have a crush on, and so on."

Her yellow-green eyes flicker with excitement. "You'll bring it tomorrow? Promise?"

I nod.

Suddenly, everyone starts whispering. I turn toward the commotion and see a woman striding along the corridor, heading toward us. She's wearing a dress with a full skirt and a red belt, looking like someone who's just stepped out of a 1950s movie.

"Who's she?" I ask the girls around me, but the woman answers for herself.

"I'm Mrs. Galka," she says. "Your new homeroom and Russian language teacher. Welcome to our class, Laura!"

She knows my name. How?

"Mr. Chaika came to talk to me this morning," she says, guessing my unspoken question.

I watch her unlock the classroom door and then follow everyone inside.

"You can sit with Hana," Mrs. Galka says, pointing to a desk on the side in front.

I look at the surprisingly tiny girl, pulling her things out of her backpack. So, this is the A student. Her expression is serious; it's as if she has all the weight of the world on her shoulders.

"Nice to meet you, Hana," I say, sitting next to her.

"Hi," she replies. "You need to prepare your workbook and textbook. The school bell will ring soon."

I grimace. I don't want her to see my workbook from my previous school. It's filled with sloppy writing.

"I heard about your parents," she almost whispers. "I'm so sorry."

I snap my head up and look at her, shocked. The silence is stretching between us while I'm trying to find my words.

"Everyone knows?" I ask.

"No." She shakes her head. "Leo only told me."

Of course he'd tell her. Sucking up to his love interest.

"Don't worry," she hurries to say. "I'm not going to tell anyone."

I believe her. No wonder all the boys have a crush on this girl. She's nice and truthful, not like me.

"Yes," I say with a sigh. "It's unfortunate that my mother broke her back while performing ballet on the stage. Now she'll have to spend months and months in the hospital."

"What?" Hana asks, gaping at me. I can almost hear her mind spinning with questions.

Fortunately, we're interrupted by two girls who've just appeared in our aisle and are standing at our desk.

"Hi, we're the Shchuka sisters, Shakira and Latifah," one of them, a short blonde, says, then points to the tall brunette at her side. "She's Shakira."

Sisters? How could they be so different then?

"Are you the girls I saw yesterday in the courtyard?" I ask them.

"Yes," Latifah says. "We live close to you. Wanna walk to school with us every day?"

I nod vigorously. "At what time do we take off?"

"Seven-thirty. Elena also lives nearby and will be walking with us."

I turn back and look at the girl Shakira is pointing to. Elena is standing on a chair, reciting some kind of funny verse to the class, making everyone roll in the aisles with laughter.

She's sobbing with laughter herself as she struggles to continue the verse. "I have green polka-dot shorts. They're great, oh, so great. Everyone asks me to show them but not you, big fool. How dare you, how dare you not to show interest! I have funny dotted shorts. Don't you understand?"

I have an attack of giggles too, and the muscles in my stomach start to hurt. I hope no one will wet themselves from laughing so hard. Elena has us all in stitches. *You go, girl!* I want to have her as my best friend.

The school bell rings, and Elena jumps from her chair, then drags it to her desk. She's the tallest girl in the class and very thin. She could be a model when she grows up.

I look back at Hana, and she's staring at me. I quickly whisper, "Don't tell anyone about my parents."

She nods and makes a zipping motion across her lips, then focuses on the teacher, waiting for her to start the class. As the teacher does start the class, I take a peek at Elena again. She continues giggling quietly into the crook of her arm. And then, throughout the class, she keeps swiveling like a propeller, chatting with everyone around her. Yes, I definitely want her as my friend.

When all the classes are over, Leo, who's been absent from my field of vision all day, suddenly reappears and gestures for me to follow him outside.

I'm surprised when he shares a bag of colorful candies he's bought at a retail kiosk. He's not stingy at all. A nice fellow.

As we're walking up the hill about halfway home, he suddenly says, "The Shchuka sisters are our neighbors. Walk with them to and from school from now on."

"You're already getting rid of me?" I ask.

"I just don't want to be dragging a girl around."

"You can start walking alone right now."

Leo smirks, then actually crosses the road to the other side and continues walking up the hill there. I roll my eyes at him. He'll have to cross back over to get into the building. Duh! And he does, humming to himself, pretending not to see me at all.

In the apartment, I bend to pet King, who's jumping and panting and can't stop turning around. Sweet, sweet boy.

After kicking my shoes off, I go to the kitchen and open the refrigerator wide, admiring the shelves stuffed with all kinds of food.

"Grandma works as a cook, remember?" Leo asks, noticing my stunned expression as he enters the kitchen behind me.

"Is she allowed to bring so much food home?" I ask.

"Yes, they have a lot of unused stuff every day. If you want to always have food in your house, become a cook."

I chuckle at his so-called wisdom and shake my head. "I'd rather become an accountant and count numbers."

"But if hard times ever come, you won't be able to eat those numbers."

My head falls back with laughter. Leo is rocking today with his humor.

I look back at him. "If you're going to be a part of the Italian Mafia, we won't have hard times, will we?"

"Who said I'd share with you?" he asks, smiling.

I shake my head at him. "You're annoying. Leave me alone."

I grab a pack of cottage cheese and a container of sour cream, close the fridge and go mix the two ingredients with sugar.

"How much cocoa powder should I put in my mug?" Leo asks. He's still here.

"Two teaspoons," I answer on a guess.

Why? Does he think that just because I'm a girl, I should know these things?

The result of my whipping the ingredients with a spoon is a yumminess worthy of the best creamy-dessert award. And with so much food in the fridge, I can eat whatever I want, whenever I want, unless Mrs. Chaika Sr. minds that, of course.

Hmm . . . there's nothing more wonderful than a good nap after a full meal. I go over to my couch and lie down.

I'm drifting off to sleep slowly, then suddenly I wake up gasping for air, as if something has just startled me or I haven't inhaled for a while. My heart is pounding. Maybe I'm going to have a heart attack and die. Should I ask Leo to call an ambulance?

I turn over on my stomach and press my chest into the couch, trying to force my heart to slow down. It does. But now my consciousness starts slipping into blankness, and just in case I never wake up again, I send God thoughts of love and gratitude. Then everything turns dark.

"Get up and do your homework." Leo's voice emerges out of nowhere.

I open my eyes and see him hovering over me in his spiffy sweatshirt with a blue dragon on it. What a pest!

"I've already done mine," he says. "Use the desk in my parents' room."

"I'll do my homework tomorrow," I say hoarsely. "I'll wake up at 4 a.m."

"That's crazy."

We both turn as the door cracks open, and Mr. Chaika enters the room. Oh wow! He's wearing a police uniform, and he has a gun holstered on his belt. I've only seen those in movies before. I look at Leo to gauge his reaction. He isn't impressed at all.

Mr. Chaika nods brusquely at us in greeting and hurries to his room, closing the door behind him.

"No desk—no homework," I announce triumphantly. Although . . . I need to do something useful, or everyone will think I'm a lazybones. I have never used a vacuum cleaner before. Will it be too noisy?

Mr. Chaika's door opens just as I get up. He comes out with a rolled-up newspaper under his arm, dressed in a homey T-shirt and shorts.

"How was your first day at school?" he asks me.

"Good," I reply, suddenly feeling shy.

He nods, then looks at Leo and back at me. "There are some children's clothes stored at the police station. I'd like the two of you to come tomorrow and see what fits."

Leo and I bob our heads eagerly. At the back of my mind, a question arises. Are those kids to whom those clothes belonged OK? Were they sent to foster families or orphanages and didn't need their old clothes anymore?

"How is Serge?" Leo asks Mr. Chaika.

"He's doing well at a juvenile offenders' institution in another city," he replies and exits into the corridor.

I turn to Leo and ask, "Who's Serge?"

"A boy who lived with us for a few days," Leo answers. "He liked to read books. He would have read all our books if he hadn't been sent to prison."

"Prison?" I shriek.

"For minors."

"And why was he living with you?"

"Dad sometimes takes in teenagers who are transitioning to . . . to . . . those institutions. You're the only one he's taken permanently."

"I hope my mom will be released soon," I say dreamily.

"I don't think so," Leo says. "There's a rumor she had a fight in jail and is facing an additional two years."

I bend over in shock. "You're kidding me, right?"

It sounds like something my mom could've done. If it's true, I hope the officers will take pity on her and won't tell the judge.

A lump in my throat starts choking me. I exit the room and head for the bathroom to cry. Of course it turns out to be occupied.

I turn around and call King to go outside with me for a walk. I'll find some quiet place to cry there. Thankfully, I don't need a key to open the front door; there's a latch rod that will give me no trouble.

I storm downstairs after King, who's leaping over several steps at a time, finding energy to also circle around me. Outside, we plunge through the grove surrounding the courtyard, and I allow King to sniff the territory all he wants while I sit under a maple tree.

I feel much better now and don't want to cry. I start playing with the fallen leaves, imagining myself as a doctor giving the leaves vaccination shots. The leaves perfectly resemble human hands, with veins and all.

When I get bored, I stand up and give King the command to follow me home. But he completely ignores me. I continue calling for him, all in vain. He's faking deafness, just like I did when the bus driver asked me for my ticket.

All King's love for me forgotten, he proceeds to walk up the hill and away from me.

"Come back, King!" I yell again, spitting out the words.

No reaction. I'm so indignant. I start stomping my foot, then run after him and grab his furry back. He still pretends I'm not even there.

From the corner of my eye, I catch sight of Varvara shimmying into the courtyard. Hooray!

"There's Varvara," I say to King, and he actually stops what he's doing and lifts his head to look back. What a disrespectful con artist.

"He wasn't obeying me," I complain as I follow King toward Varvara.

"Don't worry, he'll learn soon enough that you're one of his humans," she says encouragingly.

"But what if he gets lost? It's horrible to be lost."

"Horrible? Have you ever gotten lost?"

"Yes, for example, when I went to the Winter Theater."

"Couldn't you ask someone for help?"

"I did," I say. "But they only gave me information on where the theater was."

Varvara raises her brows. "So?"

"I knew where the *theater* was. I didn't know where *I* was!"

She drops her head back and laughs. "That must be the funniest thing I've ever heard."

I laugh with her, then notice her fishnet-clad legs.

"I want tights like yours," I cry out.

"I can buy you similar ones," she says. "But back to the theater . . . did you find your way in the end?"

"Yep, because I just continued walking straight ahead."

"And how was the show?"

"Great, but I wanted to be on the stage and dance too."

"Should we find you a dance studio then?"

"Yees, of course!" I exclaim.

"Ask your classmates about the studios they attend," she says. My heart flutters with happiness. "I will! I will!"

As we walk upstairs, I'm already creating a plan in my mind. It whirls with possibilities. I can ask Hana, the ballerina, but I like modern dance more, so I'll ask other classmates. I heard the best dance teacher in Sochi works in the concert hall Festivalny, and her name is Mrs. Shakhmatova. I need to find her phone number.

"My girlfriends want to meet you," Varvara says, unlocking the door.

I scrunch my face. "But what if they don't like me?"

"Why wouldn't they?"

"I'm stupid."

Varvara rolls her eyes at me with an indulgent smile, then says, "Go to the living room. I'll fix chocolate-butter sandwiches, and we'll watch the *Terminator* movie tonight."

Leo is sitting on the carpet, playing with Lego blocks, when I come into the living room. He seems lost in his thoughts, absorbed in creating a spaceship.

"Put away your project for today," I say. "We're going to watch a movie with Varvara."

"Then help me carry it to the cabinet," he says.

When Varvara comes with three plates of sandwiches, we sit on our couches, and she turns on the VCR. Balancing our plates on our knees, we start chewing on the yummy bread.

The movie starts, and a human-like machine goes on a mission to . . . terminate someone?

Ten minutes into the movie, Leo asks me, "Can I eat your sandwich?"

"No," I snap. "I'm chewing mine slowly so it'll last longer."

"I see," he says disappointedly and turns his attention back to the movie.

At some point Varvara falls asleep, and the remote control slips off her knees and onto the floor. I look at Leo to see if he's noticed that, but he's busy trembling. From fear? I burst out laughing.

"What?" Varvara asks, slowly waking up.

"Leo is afraid of the Terminator," I shout, pointing my finger at him. "Ninnyyy!"

He immediately jumps up from his couch and darts out into the corridor, slamming the door behind him. I stare at it in shock, not taking my eyes off it. *Seriously?*

I swallow my guilt and look at Varvara apologetically.

"He's just sensitive," she tells me reproachfully.

I nod as if I understand, but I don't. Movies aren't real. What is there to fear?

Should I go after him? As I debate, the door quietly creaks open, and Leo sneaks back in, sitting on his couch and avoiding my gaze.

Good decision. Watching a scary movie is better than standing in the corridor alone, sulking.

At ten o'clock sharp, Varvara tells us to make our beds—she's very strict about bedtime; there's no negotiating with her. I fume about that fact while I'm fluffing my pillow with too much force, then I crawl under my blanket and fall asleep.

"That's her," someone whispers in the dark.

I cringe. Someone's woken me up in the middle of the night. Couldn't they be quieter? I hate when someone does this. It reminds me of the nights Dad was drunk.

I try to fall back asleep, but the sense that someone's watching me disturbs me. I raise my head and look up.

There, in the lighted corridor, stands a petite woman with purple hair and differently colored eyes. I rub the sleep from my own eyes to see if I'm mistaken. But no, they're different. One is blue, and the other is brown. Wow, I've heard it's a sign of being a witch. Another old wives' tale, I'm sure.

"Hi," she says in a thin, husky voice. "I'm Mrs. Chaika."

Feeling too shy to reply, I lie back on my pillow and return to the arms of Morpheus. Before my mind goes blank, I hear Mrs. Chaika murmuring, "What an impolite girl."

I wake up again, but now everything is dark. Where is that woman? I need to say hello to her. I try to turn my neck, but my body is paralyzed. There's a creature sitting on my legs—a cartoon character, Leopold the Cat. Horrified, I try to move, but my body still doesn't obey me. So terrifying.

Other colorful characters start running around the room in the dark, scaring me. I need to fight them, or they'll kill me!

Mentally, I beg my body to move so I can push away Leopold the Cat, but he jumps on my chest painfully. Am I imagining all of this? Dreaming? Hallucinating? But it's so real!

Finally, the tips of my fingers start moving. I use all my will to bend them. The movement doesn't go farther than that. My head starts spinning. Everything goes blank again.

Chapter Twenty-Two
Melancholy

October, November, December . . . months are slowly passing by. Too slowly. I count every day and scratch out the dates in the calendar I've drawn. There are five years and three months left until my mom returns.

I close my eyes and think of the day Mr. Chaika and I spent in the downtown courthouse of justice, the very courthouse on the opposite side of my old apartment building. Poor Mom, being so close to home and yet unable to go there.

It was a very eventful day. First, detectives interviewed me, then I went and testified on a witness stand, answering the judge's questions. I tried to remember and tell about all the times Dad had tried to kill Mom. I couldn't help him anymore, so I helped my mother.

Mr. Chaika said later that my testimony convinced the judge to cut my mother's sentence in half. One of our neighbors, who'd seen my father chasing my mother when she was naked, also testified. Additional help came from a government-appointed psychiatrist. She deemed that my mother had been temporarily insane at the time of the crime.

Still, I almost fainted when I heard the sentence—five and a half years in Ust-Labinsk city prison. Mom's eyes were so sad; she was probably shocked too.

How will I survive without her for so long? All I want to do is sleep and not think about anything, especially after I learned more horrible bits and pieces about what Mom did. She killed Dad when she returned home to take more of our things, then she saw him sleeping with his door unlocked and used that opportunity.

She took Dad's axe from the balcony and struck him on the head fourteen times. *Fourteen times.* I cringe each time I imagine it. I hope Dad didn't have time to feel the pain.

I open my eyes like I've been burned by the memories and look out the window, letting reality melt the horrific visuals in my head.

Since court, Mr. and Mrs. Chaika have become my legal guardians. Mr. Chaika is very kind and honorable. He even tried to find my father's grave, but a funeral worker misspelled Dad's last name, and his record is lost forever. We have no idea where his grave is.

Mrs. Chaika is kind too, but not always. Not to me at least. She says I'm not the girl she was expecting me to be. Once she even threatened to send me to an orphanage. I pray every day on my way home from school for this not to happen.

Mr. Chaika defends me often, thankfully, even when I'm in the wrong. One time I was dusting the TV set and accidentally knocked over a plastic bird sitting there, breaking it. When later Mr. Chaika saw his wife barreling angrily toward me, he ran after her, shouting that it was *he* who'd broken the bird, not I. I was so grateful.

He didn't defend me the last time, though. He believed his wife when she said I'd stolen the dice from the adults' backgammon game during a party at their friends' house. And so, I'm still being punished. Why in the heck would I need those dice? Even after searching all my things and not finding anything, the Chaikas continued to believe it was me.

Varvara and Leo have distanced themselves from me too. Leo even called me a homeless bum. That really hurt. Can't all of us be friends again? I'll try to be a good sister.

So today everyone except the senior Chaikas has gone to a new party without me. How unfair!

I focus on the wide balcony windows again and look at the floating clouds. They remind me of Mrs. Chaika's kind side. She taught me how to look at the clouds and see various figures in them, such as elephants, bunnies, and dragons.

Sometimes when she's sad, Mrs. Chaika likes to talk to me for hours, telling me stories about her youth, her parents, and her romance with Mr. Chaika. They started dating at sixteen and have never been apart. He even sacrificed his early career as a soccer player to be with her.

I like listening to Mrs. Chaika. She praises me for being smart and understanding. Sometimes she asks me to sing songs, and when I do, she cries and tells me I'm talented and beautiful. I like this side of Mrs. Chaika. Deep in my heart, I know—she's coming to love me.

I smile at the good memories and look for figures in the gray clouds. I can't distinguish any. With the cherry tree, though, I can envision the figure of an anguished person tapping against the windowpanes.

Spooked, I roll out of bed and stand up. White specks appear in my eyes from the sudden movement. I wait for them to disappear, then go to the kitchen to make my first cup of black tea with a slice of lemon and lots of sugar.

Mr. Chaika's mom is in the kitchen, cooking.

"Would you like some cherry dumplings?" she asks.

"No," I reply. "I don't wanna eat. Only tea."

Besides, I still secretly don't like the way she cooks. It's a mystery to me why her daughter-in-law cooks so much better than she does. Shouldn't a professional chef cook better than anyone?

"It's up to you," she snaps. "My task is to offer; yours is to refuse."

Rude. Though it's a famous Russian saying. I smile nicely.

"If you're not going to eat," Mrs. Chaika Sr. says, "I have something to show you."

She gestures for me to wait, then goes into the bathroom with her off-balance gait and reappears with a bundle of white material.

"What's this?" she asks, shoving it in my face.

Alarm bells start ringing in my head. I recognize the material—it's my nightgown. How can I explain why it's soiled with dirt?

"Did you sneak out at night?" she asks.

Yes . . . but I'm not telling you that. After being under supervision all day long, I discovered I could slip out of the house at about 4 a.m. when everyone was sound asleep. I've been going downstairs to the courtyard and sitting on the rocks with the stray cats, who follow invisible things in the air with their eyes. People say cats can see spirits, ghosts, and angels. I don't believe that, but watching those cats following something with their big eyes was creepy.

"Don't do it again," Mrs. Chaika Sr. says, almost yelling.

"I won't," I answer reluctantly. *Not after what happened last time.* I saw a man standing at the shed behind the basketball court, watching some flames. That's when I slid into the dirt—I was trying to run away.

Later I heard it was arson. I hope no one died in that shed. Just the thought of someone dying gives me hives, especially if it's a dog dying.

Recently, I saw a German shepherd sitting at the side of the road with a dead dog. I asked our neighbors what happened, and they told me the two dogs were siblings. One of them had been run over by a car, and the other had dragged the first to the safety of the sidewalk. Since then the second dog has been sitting with the first.

"What's with your face?" Mrs. Chaika Sr. asks, suddenly looking worried.

"Nothing," I mumble.

"Your eyes look sly like a fox's eyes. Is there something else you're hiding?"

I can't roll my eyes at her—it's rude—so I close them. Poor foxes. Why do fables always paint them as conniving?

"No," I answer, opening my eyes. "And don't worry, I won't be your problem anymore."

"Are you going to behave then?" she asks.

"Why bother? I'll just commit suicide."

"What? I'm telling my son you said that."

I backtrack immediately. "I was joking. I swear!"

"Don't joke like that. And swearing is a sin."

I nod. Did she believe me that easily? I go to the stove, trying to act normal and finally begin my tea preparation.

"Are you going back to your couch?" Mrs. Chaika Sr. asks. "It's going to get a hole in it soon if you keep sitting there all day."

Leave me alone. Go away.

She does go away, but right at the door of her room, she turns and says, "We're only hard on you because we care about you."

Where's this kindness coming from? I smile at her a little, then continue making tea.

A hot mug in my hands, I lean on the windowsill and watch the people below. Music is playing from someone's window. I listen to a few notes, and my heart flutters with recognition. "Mommy for a Baby Mammoth," a song from a cartoon, is the saddest song in the world. A baby mammoth sails on an ice floe to Africa to find his mommy. On the way, he's singing, wishing for her to hear him.

I wipe the tears off my face and return to the living room. I halt at the cabinet and scan the titles of the books. *Thais of Athens* seems the least boring of all—the cover is glossy and colorful, quite modern.

I lie with it on my couch, prop my pillow up, and turn to the first pages. I read, but random thoughts keep popping into my head, sidetracking me from the sentences that become blurry.

I wrap myself tighter in the blanket and just stare pointlessly into space. The day slowly progresses, and the shadows around me become deeper. The Chaikas must be enjoying themselves to no end with their Armenian friends—dancing, playing drums, eating, and toasting each other.

The last time I attended a party like that, I danced all day, having fun. Everyone was clapping for me, even Mr. Chaika. Now I'll never have such fun again. I definitely need to end my life.

Feeling a sudden burst of energy, I jump off the couch and grab Mom's perfume vial from my drawer. There! If I drink it, the chemicals will poison me.

I lift the cap off the vial and sniff. Mmm, lilies of the valley, reminding me of spring. I heard they're also poisonous. Perfect.

I lower the vial to my mouth and tilt it over. Ugh, it burns. I drink it again, pouring the last drops into my mouth. Done.

I climb back under my blanket, curl up in a ball, and wait to die. One minute . . . two . . . three . . . The last thing I think before the darkness swallows me is I'll miss the sun, the trees, and the flowers. *God, I've changed my mind!*

God Loves Me

I see light through my closed eyelids. That means it's morning. Why is my head pounding?

I open one eye and raise myself up on my elbows to look around. Leo and Varvara are sleeping under their leopard-print blankets. Varvara's blanket is dark brown, while Leo's is orange. I was promised a similar blanket—a tiger one. Mrs. Chaika will buy it on her next business trip abroad.

I stretch my arms and yawn. The headache slowly subsides, and I have a feeling it's going to be a good day. I'll meet Elena at her house, so we'll have more time to chat on our way to school. She'll probably still be wearing her hair in African braids. A family friend—a ski champion—braided them for her. I'll finally be honest and admit how much I like them.

The memories of yesterday suddenly rush in. *Why aren't I dead?* What a miracle! I can't believe it.

A soft click of the living room door makes me turn. Mr. Chaika enters quietly, holding an envelope in his hand. He's smiling. A very unusual sight.

"Look what I have for you," he whispers so as not to wake Leo and Varvara.

I cock my head to the side and try to figure out what he means.

"This is a letter from your mother," he says.

I grab the envelope and turn away, huddling into the back of my couch and tearing the flap open. There are a double-sided sheet of paper and a handkerchief inside. The handkerchief is with a crocheted yellow sun in its middle. Only Mom could've made something beautiful like this. I lay it on my pillow and unfold the letter.

My sweet baby Laura,

I miss you so much! I want to kiss you all over.

Let me tell you about my life here. It's not easy, baby. I'm still getting used to it. Earning money in prison is difficult and takes weeks, and then I can only buy a bar of soap and a pack of cigarettes, Prima. Cigarettes in prison are like money. We, the inmates, exchange them between ourselves for other things we need.

The prison food tastes plain and rubbery. We hardly ever get meat. On the best days, we have fresh bread. And it tastes delicious.

Day in, day out, we work and work. At first, I was assigned to work in the fields, but later I was transferred to work at the clothes factory. I've been pressing the pedal of an industrial sewing machine for so long that one of my calf muscles has grown to the size of a grapefruit. You'll laugh when you see it.

Everything in prison looks unappealing—gray concrete walls, decrepit fences, barbed wire, and not a lot of greenery.

My fellow inmates are wonderful, though. Friendships can make life sweeter. One of my friends, a young lady named Eve, was recently diagnosed with tuberculosis and now has to live in an isolation ward. I help her as much as I can.

My other friend, Inessa, is from Sochi too. She was convicted of killing her spouse in self-defense and is going to be released soon. I'll give her your home phone number so the two of you can meet for a chat.

Besides spending time with friends, I like reading books. The prison has an amazing library. Also, the prison offers vocational classes, and I'm going to enroll in as many as I can handle.

Please write back soon. Sometimes I have difficulties falling asleep, worrying about you.

Love you,
Your mom

PS: If you can, insert a few postage stamps inside your envelope so I can reply to you as soon as possible too.

I kiss my mother's beautiful handwriting, put her letter next to the handkerchief, then hurry to my new Barbie backpack and take out a pen and a sheet of paper. Returning to my couch, I start to write.

Dear Mom,

I'm happy to have received your letter. I've missed you so much, but I have nothing but hope that you'll be pardoned for good behavior soon.

Mrs. Chaika was planning to send you a parcel with necessities, like shampoo and other things. Now that I know cigarettes are like money in prison, we'll buy them for you.

I have new friends too. My bestie is my classmate, Elena. She is sincere and kind and looks almost like my twin sister, except she's fair-haired. We hang out for hours after school, and she always shares half of her treats and pocket money with me.

Doll and Mickey—you won't believe it—returned from the tea plantation to our courtyard and now live there. I'll never know how they managed to find their way over twenty miles. I hope our neighbors feed them, as Mr. Chaika didn't allow me to take them to live with us.

Here is the most important news—Mr. Chaika's wife promised to take me on a train to visit you next summer before Leo (their son) and I go to summer camp in Volgograd.

In school, I like English as a foreign language and math. I don't like geography. The teacher makes my heart race with fear. Everyone's afraid of her. One kid even called the principal anonymously and lied that there was a bomb in the school.

I once pretended my stomach hurt so I could stay home, but something went awry, and Mrs. Chaika took me to the hospital. The doctors thought I had appendicitis and hospitalized me for two weeks. Please don't tell anyone I told you this.

My homeroom teacher, Mrs. Galka, likes how I dance, so now she makes me perform in all our school events. I'm soon starting dance classes at the theater opposite the police station. Do you remember it?

In the evenings, I enjoy walking with the Chaikas' dog, King. We often sit high on a deserted cliff and watch the city lights below. I don't know about King, but I enjoy the peace and quiet there.

One of my neighbor friends, Julia, recently gave me a book about God, and I went to church to ask the priest to baptize me. He told me to choose my godparents first and come later. I'll ask the Chaikas.

One more thing: when you return from prison, I want us to repair our apartment so it'll be white and light and beautiful as candy.

Oh, and that reminds me . . . the government wanted to take away our apartment, but Mr. Chaika didn't allow it. He'll help me privatize it so it'll belong to me.

I'll wait for your next letter like a flower for the rain.

Yours,
Laura

I put my pen down, hug myself with glee, and sigh contentedly. I still feel homesick, but at least now I have some kind of connection to my mother.

I get up and go look for Mr. Chaika. He's in the kitchen, eating Abkhazian mandarins.

"How's your mother?" he asks.

"Good," I reply shyly. I always clamp up when he's talking to me.

"Do you need an envelope to write back to her?"

I nod. "And some stamps for me and for Mom."

He nods and goes to his bedroom, where Mrs. Chaika is sleeping soundly. I follow after him and watch as he opens the cabinet with well-organized black folders. I zero in on a stack of postage stamps there. A thought flits through my mind—should I take some more stamps later? *No!* I'll never ever steal again. I won't even touch something that doesn't belong to me.

"Are you going to the post box now?" Mr. Chaika asks as he hands me the supplies.

"Yes," I reply and walk over to my couch.

Following Mom's example, I decide to add things to the envelope. I put my best drawing of flowers and my most recent photo together with my letter, then copy both addresses from Mom's envelope to mine and seal the flap. All done.

Once I'm outside, I realize I don't really know where the post boxes are. I decide to just run along the street and see if I can find one along the way. I'm in luck. A shiny blue post box is standing proudly on the corner of the grocery store.

Exhilarated, I cross the road, ignoring passersby's stares at my PJs. *No, I'm not cold.*

I touch the metal post box and peek inside. It's not overfilled, good. I slip my letter carefully through the slot and spin around in joy. Growing up without my parents will be tough, but I can imagine that God is my parent, surely. He loves me. And no one will ever take him away from me. It's just that simple—I'll never be alone.

Epilogue
Happily Ever After

My fiancé Timothy and I are strolling down Voykova Street toward the home of my childhood. He's finally going to meet my mother in person. I'm so nervous. Will he like her the way she is?

Today is the warmest day of October 2021 so far. Sunlight is flickering through the trees, reaching leaves on the ground in a series of gentle waves. Fall is all about the beauty of nature. And nostalgia.

We turn into the driveway, and I point out the garden on our left.

"The cherry tree," I say excitedly. "The one I climbed when I was little."

Timothy nods with a smile.

Celine Dion song, "My Heart Will Go On," is playing from someone's window. How apt—it always makes me think of my father.

I sigh with a sweet remembrance and focus on the courtyard ahead. In the past, it resembled a botanical garden; now it looks more like a parking lot—only a few palm trees are left, and no flowers.

"I wish Elena could come to the US for our wedding," Timothy says.

I sigh. "The US Embassy and consulates in Russia have suspended immigrant visa services indefinitely, with all the—"

"Yes," Timothy replies. "But maybe she can get a visa from another country? I'll pay for her tickets."

His gentle voice makes me feel happy. He speaks like a teacher or a preacher, in a calm, kind way. His serenity balances me and holds me steady.

His looks aren't quiet, though. The kids in Russia follow him around whenever they see him, asking if he's a Hollywood actor. I can definitely see why. With his deep golden skin, athletic physique, and curly black hair, he looks very unusual for our region. And when he wears his black shades, oh my . . .

Timothy nudges me to answer his question. What was it? Ah, visas!

"My daughter and I will go to Israel to get our visas," I say. "Going through so much would be next to impossible for Elena."

"Well, the most important thing is that your daughter Amina will be with us," he says. "And she'll be your bridesmaid."

"And your son will be your groomsman. How sweet is this?"

Timothy chuckles. "*Our* son. *Our* daughter. Would you have liked for your mom and foster parents to come?"

"Maybe, but you're right about Elena. She and her mom are the two people I really want at my wedding."

Elena and her saint of a mother have been two angels in the lives of my daughter and me. When I got pregnant at nineteen, they took me in and helped me care for my little baby.

Another person I'd have liked to have at my wedding is Mimosa. A Georgian woman with smiling eyes, she came into my life as a housekeeper but has become so much more. She helped me raise my daughter in good and bad times.

As for my mom, I left our apartment when I was eighteen after she threatened me with a knife. She loves me very deeply, but after she returned from prison, her nerves weren't healthy. And my teenage rebelliousness didn't help.

Timothy squeezes my hand. "What are you thinking about?"

"Uh, just remembering," I reply, squeezing back.

As we round the building, we see my mother already waiting for us on the porch, smiling. I snicker to myself. She's dressed in a blue zippered dress with the words "Wild Love" embroidered on the material.

"I'm so happy to meet you," she gushes, taking a giant step toward Timothy.

"And I'm honored to meet you, Mrs. Talia," he replies, hugging her warmly.

Mom leans into his embrace affectionately, then turns to me and mouths, "He's surprisingly attractive."

"Mother!" I yelp, covering my face with my palms, but still translate it into English for Timothy.

He laughs. "Thank you, Mrs. Talia, thank you!"

Mom gestures for us to go into the apartment, then ushers us into the living room that once was Dad's room. Seating us on the couch, she gracefully settles into the armchair opposite us and starts to talk. And boy, can she talk! Smartly enough, she gives me plenty of time to translate.

"I told Victor to take a stroll while you're here," she says, "so he wouldn't be in the way."

As I translate this to Timothy, his eyes widen, so I hurry to explain, "She doesn't mean my father, no. Her boyfriend has the same name."

And it's not the only similarity. Mom told me he also liked to drink. But what's not similar between them is their age difference. Mom's boyfriend is almost my age. I have no idea how they've managed to live together for fourteen years.

My gaze stops on a beautiful bouquet of daisies on a rectangular table near the wall. I take a moment to scan the room further. Mom has remodeled most of the apartment, but everything still seems the same, only the smell of mold has become stronger.

I return my attention to Mom. Her face is wrinkled and pale—a hard life is written all over it. But she still has no gray hair. *Go figure.*

"Translate," Timothy says, nudging me.

"You don't have to," Mom protests, looking at me. "I understand English perfectly. When I was young, I spoke it fluently, just like you."

To demonstrate her skills, she singsongs in English, "*Wonderful, wonderful!*"

Timothy and I look at each other, and sparks of humor fly between us.

Timothy turns back to Mom. "Yes, Mrs. Talia, your English is perfect."

Mom nods, pretending to understand what he said. Only a sideways glance at me betrays that she's waiting for my translation. When I do translate the compliment, her eyes widen with pleasure.

She fixes her gaze back on Timothy and says in Russian, "I lived in America in the past."

Oh, Mother. She's starting to weave her fantasies. Again, she watches me out of the corner of her eye, waiting for me to translate.

Timothy looks at Mom tenderly. "Did you like America?"

"Yes, of course," she replies merrily, basking in his attention. "My African American boyfriend and I were building a house there."

Timothy glances at me with a conspiratorial grin. He knows what Mom's doing. Her fantasies about her boyfriend are obviously inspired by *him,* as *he's* an African American.

"Did you finish building the house?" he asks Mom. He's playing along with her. *How sweet.*

"No," Mom answers sadly. "I had to leave for China."

Timothy squeezes my knee, and I put my hand on his. I'm in awe of him. There's no other man in the world who'd have been more accepting of my mother. He even prays for her in the evenings.

Mom, the fantasy-weaver, continues her story. "I went on a concert tour there as a violin player in an orchestra."

I press a palm to my lips and try not to laugh. Timothy is more successful with that; only a handsome smile is slowly creeping toward his ears.

Mom doesn't give us time to recover. She continues, "The work in the orchestra was boring. I once fell asleep during a performance and tumbled down into the orchestra pit, together with my violin."

All three of us burst out laughing. How could anyone invent such an intricate story? I'll never know if Mom genuinely believes what she tells us or if she knows she's making it all up. In any scenario, she has a fantastic imagination.

"Would you like some tea?" Mom asks us, remembering the rules of hospitality. "I have candies."

"No, thank you," I hurry to answer. "We need to go home."

"What a pity!"

I give her an apologetic smile and stand up. Timothy stands up too, and suddenly, his expression turns serious.

"Mrs. Talia," he says, "I love your daughter and would like to ask your blessing to marry her."

"Yes, of course," Mom immediately replies, not surprised by his American formality.

"Thank you so much, Mrs. Talia," Timothy says, clasping her hands.

"You're so lucky to have Sasha . . . um . . . Laura," Mom says shamelessly. "She was the smartest kid on the planet."

"Mom, stop," I interject. Secretly, though, I'm flattered.

"Are you sure you don't want tea?" Mom asks us.

"Positive. We ate recently."

"May we take a picture with you?" Timothy asks Mom.

She gasps. "I don't have my brows drawn on today."

I chuckle. "We'll add them in Photoshop." *Maybe.*

All three of us stand with our backs to the glass balcony and direct our gazes to Timothy's smartphone as he takes a few pictures of us.

He shows them to Mom for her approval, and she sighs dreamily. "You kids look so young."

Timothy's and my eyes meet, and I try not to giggle. Mom has no idea he's actually older than me. All his time spent in his basement gym and running marathons around Washington, DC, has paid off.

"I'm still going to give you the candies," Mom says and turns toward her bedroom.

Timothy shoves a handful of bills into my hand. "Give it to her."

"Here's some money for you, Mom," I say, walking after her.

She looks at the money and turns to Timothy. "Thank you, thank you! You can't imagine how much it is for me!"

"You're most welcome, Mrs. Talia," he replies humbly.

"I'll bring you some gifts too," she says and scurries into her bedroom.

Timothy and I slowly walk into the corridor and wait for Mom there. I look at the bedroom door. It still has axe marks scattered over it, deeply scarring the wood.

I tug Timothy closer and touch the marks with my fingers. "Do you remember I told you about them?"

His face crumbles, and he draws me into a hug.

"A kiss in the house of your childhood?" he asks.

I pucker my lips.

At this moment, the bedroom door suddenly flies open, and something metal rockets across the floor. Timothy flinches.

I narrow my eyes at him playfully. "Afraid of Russians, eh?"

"You can say that," he replies with a chuckle.

"Sorry," Mom shouts from her room. "I dropped a brooch on the floor and knocked it with my foot."

A second later, she comes into the corridor, carrying colorful candies, a book wrapped in clear plastic, and a knife. *A knife?*

She starts sticking the candies in Timothy's pockets, and I can't help my snort of amusement. The health freak that he is, he'd never eat anything with sugar. *But I will.*

"And this is the book *The Three Musketeers*," Mom says, placing it in Timothy's hands.

I immediately remember the stacks of books in her room. About five years ago, scammers promised her she'd win one million rubles if she bought just another set of books. There was always "just another set of books" to buy, and they eventually filled the room to the ceiling. At least Mom introduced Amina to the Harry Potter series, opening her life to the world of Hogwarts and all its students.

"This is a collectible souvenir knife," Mom says, continuing with her gift-giving. "It's embossed with handcrafted art."

"As an artist, I love art," Timothy says, taking the knife.

"You work as an artist?" Mom asks, looking giddy with excitement.

"He works for the federal government," I say. "But he still sells his paintings online. He's very hardworking. He even worked when he was a young teen to help his mother, who had twelve kids to support."

"That's our boy," Mom says proudly, pressing into his shoulders.

I focus on the book in Timothy's hands. How does Mom expect him to read it when it's in Russian?

"Mrs. Talia, I promise to learn Russian and read this book," Timothy says, as if sensing my question.

My mother grins at him, and he does too, looking at her adoringly.

I pull him by the elbow. "Let's go."

"But you didn't tell me about my granddaughter," Mom whines.

"She's well, studying at a university in Saint Petersburg to become a veterinarian," I tell her.

"But I thought she'd become a dancer. She danced in your school all those years and won awards in Paris."

"She's welcome to pursue as many professions as she wants, Mom."

"And I'm going to pursue investing."

"Oh dear."

"We'll finally become millionaires."

Double oh dear. Mom's obsession with becoming a millionaire is funny, yes, but I suddenly realize how strong her dream is. She's been talking about it since I was little. For the first time, I wish too that her dream would one day come true.

As we walk out of the apartment, Mom continues chatting about investing, buying bank stocks, and getting strong returns. On the porch, Timothy gives her another hug, and then he and I walk downstairs to the path below.

I pause there and touch the rough wall of the building I probably touched many times when I was a kid. It feels like I can touch the fingertips of that little *Sasha*.

"Let me take a picture of you here," Timothy says.

"OK," I agree. "But can you throw away the knife?"

"Of course not! It's a gift from Mama."

"Knives scare me. Besides, you can't take it on the plane."

I gently ease the knife from his stack of gifts and march to the trash can in the courtyard to drop it in. Then I return to his side and stand still while he taps the shutter button on his phone camera.

"Давай купим мороженое по дороге домой?" I ask as we start strolling toward my car.

"I don't speak Russian yet," he says dryly.

I start laughing. "I'm confusing languages again. I said, 'Let's buy ice cream on our way home.'"

"And a yogurt with blueberries for me."

"Okey dokey."

I have such a nice feeling. Can I grab hold of this moment and freeze time? At least for a millisecond? Or is it always either the past or the future?

The fresh evening breeze blows across my face, lifting my hair in all directions. I catch a few locks with my left hand and twirl them into one spiraling curl. Holding it tight, I focus on my engagement ring. Engraved in Old Slavic are the words:

God, please save us and keep us safe.

www.ingramcontent.com/pod-product-compliance
Lightning Source LLC
Chambersburg PA
CBHW022059090426
42743CB00008B/655